THE LITTLE BOOK OF
RANGERS

A RANGERS A to Z

Written by Graham Betts

THE LITTLE BOOK OF
RANGERS

This edition first published in the UK in 2007
By Green Umbrella

© Green Umbrella Publishing 2007

www.greenumbrella.co.uk

Publishers Jules Gammond & Vanessa Gardner

Printed and bound in Poland

ISBN-13: 978-1-905009-89-3

Contents

Advocaat

ADVOCAAT

ABOVE Dick Advocaat signals from the bench

RIGHT Dick Advocaat celebrates after the Scottish FA Cup final against Aberdeen in 2000

BORN IN THE HAGUE ON 27 September 1947, Dick Advocaat had a largely uneventful career as a player but made his mark later as a coach, commencing this side of his career at amateur side DVSP. After two spells assisting the Dutch national team he was appointed national coach in 1992 and guided the side to the World Cup finals in 1994, where they reached the quarter-finals before being beaten by Brazil.

Upon returning to Holland Dick took over at PSV Eindhoven and enjoyed four success-laden years and ended Ajax's period of domination of the domestic game. In June 1998 he was appointed manager of Rangers, replacing the previous incumbent Walter Smith. Dick's appointment was seen by many as an attempt by Rangers to translate their domestic success into European competition, for despite hav-ing competed in the European Champions Cup for ten of the previous eleven campaigns, they had only once made any real impact. Dick's reputation as one of the top coaches in Europe was expected to change all of that.

A treble in his first season in charge proved that it was business as usual on the domestic front, even though Rangers slid out of the UEFA Cup in the third round. The following season saw Rangers clinch the double and, in their return to the European Champions League, record home and away victories over PSV Eindhoven even though they were unable to progress beyond the group stage and went out of the UEFA Cup on penalties in the third round.

The 2000-01 season was a disappointing one that finished barren trophy-wise and Rangers fifteen points adrift of their

greatest rivals Celtic at the top of the Premier League. After qualifying for the Champions League that season Rangers made an impressive start, winning their opening two matches, but only two further points were secured and Rangers were eliminated, also losing their UEFA Cup tie with FC Kaiserslautern.

In December 2001 Dick Advocaat stepped down as manager of the club, to be replaced by Alex McLeish, but remained at Ibrox as director of football. Six months later he left the club entirely and returned to Holland to take over as national coach for a second time, guiding them to the semi-finals of the 2004 European Championships. He later had a spell coaching at club level in Germany before returning to the international stage, taking over as South Korean coach and taking them to the 2006 World Cup finals.

Albertz

BORN IN MÖNCHENGLADBACH on 29 January 1971, Jorg was a youth and apprentice player with PSV

Mönchengladbach and Borussia Mönchengladbach before signing his first professional contract with Fortuna Dusseldorf in 1990. Following the club's relegation to Division Two of the Bundesliga, Jorg was sold to SV Hamburg where he made his reputation, earning the nickname 'The Hammer' in recognition of his long range shooting abilities and becoming club captain after two years.

In 1996 Walter Smith paid £4 million to bring the relatively unknown German to Ibrox Park, but he soon had the crowd on his side, especially after a stunning free kick against Celtic in January 1997 that proved to be the catalyst to Rangers securing the League title for the ninth time in a row. Whilst Jorg had been a virtual ever-present whilst Walter Smith was manager, the arrival of Dick Advocaat saw Jorg slip down the pecking order, and whilst he would ultimately collect medals for winning the championship in 1997, 1999 and 2000, it was plain that he was not part of Advocaat's long term plans. A £3.5 million fee took him back to SV Hamburg in 2001, having netted 82 goals for the Light Blues during his time with the club.

Amoruso

BORN IN BARI ON 28 JUNE 1971, Lorenzo Amoruso began his career with Bari and played for Mantova, Pescara and AC Fiorentina before joining Rangers for £5 million in May 1997, although he would have to wait until the following March before he made his League debut in the 2-1 defeat by Motherwell. Lorenzo became a more regular fixture in the side during the 1998-99 season and would go on to collect a total of nine winners' medals with the club, including three Premiership titles (1999, 2000 and 2003), the Scottish Cup in 1999, 2002 and 2003 and the Scottish League Cup in 1999, 2002 and 2003. A functional and uncompromising defender during his time at Ibrox, he made the occasional foray into the opponents' half of the field and netted his first goal for the club in October 1998 against Dundee United.

His Rangers career survived allegations that he had made racist remarks towards an opponent during a European tie against Borussia Dortmund in 1999 and he remained a Ger until July 2003 when a £1.4 million deal took him to Blackburn Rovers. Rangers obviously got the best out of Lorenzo Amoruso, for his time at Ewood Park has been blighted by injuries.

ABOVE Lorenzo Amoruso celebrates with the Scottish FA Cup trophy after the Scottish FA Cup final match against arch-rivals Celtic

Attendances

These figures are Rangers' best attendances at Ibrox Stadium in each of the major competitions.

Competition	v	Date	Att
Scottish League	Celtic	1/1/1939	118,730
Scottish FA Cup	Hibernian	10/2/1951	102,342
Scottish League Cup	Celtic	16/10/1948	105,000
Europe	St Etienne	4/9/1957	85,000
	AC Milan	27/11/1957	85,000
	Leeds United	26/3/1968	85,000

Baxter

ALTHOUGH JIM BAXTER WAS A childhood Rangers fan, he began his career with Raith Rovers on a part-time basis whilst working as first a carpenter and then a collier. It was his abilities on the field, however, that attracted interest from bigger clubs, with Rangers enabling him to fulfil his childhood dream when they paid £17,500 in June 1960.

Jim was just 20 years of age at the time (he was born in Hill o' Beath in Fife on 29 September 1939) but marched straight into the first team, helping Rangers win the Scottish League and League Cup double at the end of his first season. There were to be a further two League titles, two League Cups and three victories in the Scottish FA Cup during the five years Jim was at Ibrox, a time when he was acknowledged as one of the most skilful players in the game. And yet

ABOVE Rangers captain Jim Baxter, shouldered by teammates, holds aloft the Scottish League Cup, which they won at Hampden Park by beating Celtic 2-1

the general consensus was that Jim's talent was largely allowed to go to waste, with his disinterest in training, tactics, discipline and just about everything else that goes to make a great player, all too often apparent. On his day, on the field, he could be breathtaking, none more so than his performance in the darker blue

spot with the first penalty he'd ever taken in his life.

Unfortunately most of his days off the field were spent drinking, womanising and gambling, with his physical condition suffering as a result. He was sold to Sunderland for £72,500 in May 1965 but failed to make much of an impact, although the club were able to recoup their money when they sold him to Nottingham Forest two years later for £100,000. Jim returned to Ibrox in 1969 but was not even a shadow of his former self and retired from the game in 1970 in order to become a publican.

Jim was later asked if the sums modern players were earning would have made any difference to his lifestyle, to which he replied 'Definitely. I'd have spent £50,000 a week at the bookies instead of £100.' And yet Jim is still fondly remembered, both by those who follow Rangers, who claim he was the most skilful left-half the club ever had, and by those who follow the national side, who bombarded the poll organised by Radio Five Live with nominations to get the new Wembley footbridge named after him! Jim Baxter, who won 34 caps for his country, died from cancer after a long battle on 14 April 2001.

shirt of Scotland in 1963 against England, when he inspired ten-man Scotland (his Rangers team-mate Eric Caldow suffered a broken leg) to a 2-1 victory, scoring the first from the penalty

Butcher

BORN IN SINGAPORE ON 28 December 1958, Terry was brought up in Suffolk and was spotted by Ipswich Town playing youth football in Lowestoft. Signed by the club in August 1976 he helped them win the UEFA Cup in 1981 and was first capped by England in 1980. By 1986 he was widely regarded as the best centre-half in England and was the subject of intense transfer speculation, finally joining Graeme Souness's Ibrox revolution for £725,000 in August 1986.

Alongside fellow English recruits Chris Woods and Graham Roberts, Terry galvanised a Rangers side that had lived in their rival Celtic's shadow for too long, helping them win the Scottish League in 1987, 1989 and 1990 and the Scottish League Cup in three successive seasons, 1987, 1988 and 1989. By the time of the 1990 World Cup he was acknowledged as one of the best centre-backs in the world, a reputation he enhanced during the tournament, captaining the side to the semi-finals in the enforced absence of Bryan Robson.

A few months later the end came to his Rangers career, Terry losing out after an argument with manager Graeme Souness and being sold to Coventry City in November 1990 where he eventually became player-manager. He finished his playing career with Sunderland and eventually returned to Scotland where he became manager of Motherwell – in the final match of the 2004-05 season his side beat Celtic 2-1 thus gifting the League Championship to Rangers!

ABOVE Terry Butcher holds the trophy aloft after the Skol Cup final against Celtic in 1986

Buffel

BORN IN RUDDERVOORDE, BELGIUM on 19 February 1981, Thomas Buffel began his career with Ruddervoorde and Cercle Brugge before moving on to Feyenoord during the 1999-2000 season. Able to play in midfield or up front, Thomas was sent out to Feyenoord's feeder club Excelsior Rotterdam for two years and returned to Feyenoord looking to secure a regular first team place. He reportedly fell out with the then manager Ruud Gullit over his refusal to sign a new contract and was promptly sold to Rangers in January 2005 for £2.5 million.

Despite the circumstances surrounding his arrival at Ibrox Thomas proved a worthwhile acquisition, helping the club win the Premier League and League Cup at the end of the season and being one of the star performers in the final against Motherwell. The following term he proved to be one of the few successes in an otherwise disappointing season for Rangers, Europe notwithstanding. He helped the club reach the knockout stages of the UEFA Champions League and scored seven League goals during the campaign, a good return for a midfield player. The Belgian international (he currently has 25 caps to his name) is expected to be one of the players around whom Paul Le Guen builds his version of Rangers.

Cairns

BORN IN MERRYTON ON 30 October, 1890 Tommy Cairns would go on to be a vital member of the Rangers side either side of the First World War but for some reason only won six full caps for Scotland, a meagre figure given his worth to his club. Tommy had begun his career in junior football with Burnbank Athletic and Larkhall Thistle before being lured south of the border to sign for Bristol City in 1911, but after only eleven appearances returned to Scotland to sign for Peebles Rovers. He then had a brief spell with St Johnstone before finally being spotted by Rangers and joined the Ibrox outfit in November 1913, almost immediately ensconced as first choice inside-left, a position he was to

ABOVE Tommy Cairns

hold for the next 13 years.

Tommy's time at Ibrox would be rewarded with championship medals in 1918, 1920, 1921, 1923, 1924 and 1925, although he was unable to pick up a winners' medal in the Scottish Cup, having to settle for the runners-

up variety in 1921 and 1922. All six of Tommy's international caps were awarded whilst he was associated with Rangers, the first coming in 1920, by which time he had formed an extremely effective left-wing partnership for both club and country with Alex Morton.

Tommy remained at Ibrox until 1927, having made over 400 League appearances for the club, and returned to England to play for Bradford City, making 135 appearances for the Bantams before retiring in 1932. He later served Arsenal as their chief scout in Scotland before his death in 1967.

Caldow

BORN IN CUMNOCK ON 14 MAY 1934, Eric Caldow was fortunate enough to play in two great Rangers sides, at either end of his Ibrox career. Although Eric began his association with the club at the age of 14, he was sent out to Muirkirk Juniors in order to develop his talent and was eventually recalled to Ibrox at the age of 18. The following season he made his debut in the League Cup win over Ayr United and would go on to make eight appearances for the club that term. In 1954-55 he made 11 League appearances and thereafter was a first team regular, going on to collect championship medals in 1956, 1957, 1959, 1961 and 1963.

Initially used as a right-back, Eric was later successfully converted to left-back, but it did not matter where he played, his speed, both in thought and deed, were sufficient to enable him to get the better of almost any opponent. Eric was just as regular a player for Scotland, collecting his first cap in May 1957 against Spain and going on to collect 40 before a serious leg break brought his international career to an end. It almost did for his club career too, for Eric struggled back into the side and made just three appearances during the 1963-64 season. He recovered sufficiently

BELOW The England and Scotland captains, Norman Haynes and Eric Caldow respectively, lead their teams onto the pitch at Wembley at the start of the England-Scotland match, 1961

ABOVE A jubilant
Rangers team lead by
Eric Caldow (with
Trophy) after beating
Hearts 3-1 in the
League Cup final

to make 26 League appearances the following term, but it was in the League Cup
that he enjoyed his finest moments that
term, winning a third winners' medal in
that competition to go with two in the
Scottish Cup. Eric finally brought his
playing career to an end at the end of the
1965-66 season, having made 407
appearances for the club – he wasn't
booked in any of them.

Cooper

BORN IN HAMILTON ON 25
February 1956, Davie began his professional career with Clydebank and
proved an instant success, helping the
club win successive promotions and a
place in the Premier League by the end
of the 1976-77 season. His performances on the wing for Clydebank had
not gone unnoticed by either the international selectors or scouts from bigger
clubs, for he was drafted into the
Scottish squad for the Home
International championships and summer tour of South America and became
the subject of intense transfer speculation. It eventually cost Rangers
£100,000 to secure his signature in June
1977, but it proved to be money well
spent as Davie ended his first season at
Ibrox having helped the club win the
domestic treble.

Although Celtic finished the following term Champions, Rangers retained
both cups, with Davie seemingly reserv-
ing his most effective performances for
the cup campaigns. Season 1979-80 saw
Rangers finish empty-handed amid
speculation that all was not well between

manager John Greig and his star winger,
with Davie's laid back attitude both on
and off the pitch completely at odds
with the style Greig had shown as a

ABOVE Davie Cooper
in action

ABOVE Cooper takes on Paul McStay of Celtic during the 1986 Skol Cup final at Hampden Park, Rangers won the match 2-1

RIGHT Davie Cooper in action during a match against St Johnstone

player. Brighton came in with an offer for both Davie and Gordon Smith, but Greig allowed only Smith to make the move south.

His Rangers career might have been saved but it was not entirely resurrected, for Davie was in and out of the side during the 1980-81 season. His greatest performance came in the Scottish Cup final replay against Dundee United when he virtually tore United apart on his own. Against the same opponents the following season, this time in the League Cup

Final, Davie was again the difference between victory and defeat, proof that with him in the side Rangers were a force to be reckoned with.

After another barren season in 1982-83 John Greig made way for the returning Jock Wallace, the manager who had originally signed Davie and who played him more regularly, and whilst the League title proved elusive, there were still victories in the League Cup in 1984 and 1985 to savour.

Davie was to collect a further two

League Cup winners' medals whilst with Rangers, in 1987 and 1988, scoring in both finals, by which time the manager at Ibrox had changed once again, with Graeme Souness taking the hot seat. He too began to use Davie sparingly and eventually he was transferred to Motherwell for £50,000 in August 1989. He had won three League titles, three Scottish Cups and seven League Cups whilst at Ibrox and still hadn't finished his trophy collection, adding a further Scottish Cup in 1991.

In December 1993 he returned to Clydebank, combining playing with coaching duties with the intention of retiring from playing at the end of the 1994-95 season in order to concentrate on coaching full time. Sadly, he was to suffer a brain haemorrhage whilst he and former Celtic player Charlie Nicholas were recording a coaching video for young people and died on 23 March 1995. In the immediate aftermath of his death, supporters of virtually all clubs in Scotland lay scarves in homage to Davie at Ibrox, including more than a fair few of Celtic, recognition of his accomplishments in the dark blue jersey of Scotland (he won 22 caps) as well as the light blue of Rangers.

Dawson

RIGHT Scotland goalkeeper Jerry Dawson and Germany goalkeeper Hans Jakob pictured during training at Ibrox

ONE OF THE GREATEST goalkeepers the club ever signed, Jerry Dawson proved good enough to displace another Rangers legend in Tom Hamilton and was virtually unrivalled as the number one at the club from 1933 to 1945 and would go on to win 14 full caps for his country.

Born in Falkirk in 1909, Jerry joined Rangers in 1929 and made his debut in January 1931 against St Mirren and would go on to collect five League championship and two Scottish Cup winners' medals. His tally in the latter might have been higher, for having helped Rangers reach the final in 1934 he was replaced by Tom Hamilton in the final against St Mirren!

Although proper League football was suspended for the duration of the Second World War, Jerry did help Rangers win two Scottish War Cups, two Summer War Cups and the Southern League Cup on one occasion. In 1944 he again helped Rangers to the final of the Southern League Cup but suffered a broken leg in the match that saw Hibernian win 6-5 on corners. Although the leg break was considered career threatening he returned to the side in 1945 and went on to appear in the prestigious friendly against Dinamo Moscow. This proved to be virtually the end of his Rangers career, for he moved on to Falkirk soon after and spent four years at the club before retiring in 1949. He died on 19 January 1977.

De Boer

BORN IN HOORN, HOLLAND ON 15 May 1970, the twin brother of one-time fellow Rangers player Frank, Ronald played amateur football for De Zouaven and Lutjebroek before commencing his professional career with Ajax in 1988. After three years with Ajax and never regarded as a regular, he switched to FC Twente and spent two years with the club, enhancing his reputation as a midfield player of considerable note. He returned to Ajax in 1992 and became a key component in the side that would win the UEFA Champions League in 1995.

A move to Barcelona followed in 1998 but he was used sparingly at the Nou Camp, prompting a £4.2 million swoop by Rangers in 2000, joining a growing number of Dutch internationals who could be found at Ibrox at the time. He helped the club win the domestic treble in 2002-03, scoring vital goals in all three competitions, including one in the final day 6-1 League victory over Dunfermline that enabled Rangers to take the title on goal difference.

Injuries were to blight Ronald's 2003-04 season, which saw brother Frank also arrive at Ibrox, and at the end of the campaign Ronald was told his contract would not be renewed. He moved on to Qatar where he signed for Al-Rayyan.

BELOW Ronald de Boer with the winning trophy after the 2002 Tennents Scottish Cup final between Celtic and Rangers

Drummond

ONE OF THE FIRST GREAT FULL-backs the club ever had, Jock Drummond formed an extremely useful club partnership with Nicol Smith, immediately in front of the equally impressive goalkeeper Matt Dickie.

Jock was born in Alva in 1870 and began his career with Falkirk, earning the first of his 14 Scottish caps with the club

BELOW Rangers 1896-1897 squad pose with the trophies they won during the season (fourth left in front row)

before switching to Rangers in March 1892. He did not have to wait long before collecting his first honour, helping Rangers win the Scottish Cup in 1894 with victory over Celtic. There were further cup successes in 1897, 1898 and 1903, but it was the League that was the prime concern, and that took a little longer to arrive back at the club. Although the trophy did arrive at Ibrox in 1899, Jock sat out most of the season owing to injury and so missed out on a medal, but more than adequate compensation was received when the League was retained in 1900, 1901 and 1902.

A no-nonsense defender, who favoured the immediate boot out of danger rather than dwelling on the ball looking for a colleague, Jock was known for wearing a cloth cap whilst playing! He ended his connection with Rangers in 1904 and returned to Falkirk to serve as a coach, later becoming a director of the club before his death in 1935.

English

SAM ENGLISH GAVE GOOD SERVICE
to a number of clubs during his career
but is seemingly forever remembered
for his part in the incident that led to
the death of Celtic goalkeeper John
Thomson. An official enquiry into the
incident absolved Sam of any blame, a
decision that was supported by the
Thomson family and players from both
sides who had taken part in the match,
although this did not stop crowds from
jeering him from then on.

Sam had been born in Crivolea in
County Antrim on 18 August 1908 and
moved to Scotland with his family in
1924, subsequently going on to work for
John Brown & Company and turning
out for Yoker Athletic in the non-League
game. He joined Rangers in July 1931
and enjoyed a goalscoring debut for the
club, netting twice in the 4-1 win over
Dundee and ten days later hitting five in

the 7-3 win against Morton.

On 5th September came the first
clash of the season with Celtic at Ibrox,
with the visitors unbeaten and the hosts
having suffered just one defeat. The two

ENGLISH

sides effectively cancelled each other out throughout much of the match, but five minutes into the second half Sam was sent clear by a pass from Jimmy Fleming and bore down on the Celtic goal. Goalkeeper John Thomson, as brave a goalkeeper as could be found plying his trade, rushed out to meet the danger and dived at Sam's feet just as the forward was making to shoot. Although Thomson managed to block the shot, his momentum carried him onto Sam's knee and there was a collision between the two players. Whilst Sam managed to limp away from the incident, Thomson lay stunned on the ground. Several players, including Sam, realised that Thomson was seriously hurt and frantically waved for medical assistance for the goalkeeper, who was eventually carried off the field with his head covered in bandages and taken immediately to the Victoria Infirmary. He had suffered a depressed fracture of the skull and despite frantic surgery died later that evening from his injuries.

The football world was stunned, with twenty thousand lining the route for his funeral. A later enquiry into the incident found that Thomson's own momentum had been wholly responsible for causing the damage and that should have been the end of the matter, but an ill-chosen comment from Celtic manager Willie Maley – 'I hope it was an accident' – would eventually return to haunt Sam English. Although he was to

ther ten goals the following term as Rangers won the title, but constant jeering by opposition crowds was beginning to take effect.

Sam left Rangers for Liverpool in 1933 and would score 25 goals in 47 appearances for the Anfield club. He briefly returned to Scotland to play for Queen of the South but found he was still the target for malicious chanting and so returned to England again, this time to play for Hartlepool United before finishing his career with Duntocher Hibernian and retiring from the game at the age of just 28.

He was later diagnosed with motor neurone disease and admitted to the Vale of Leven Hospital at the age of 58. According to one nurse who attended him, he appeared to be an old man well before his time, the events of September 1931 having haunted him for the rest of his life, which came to an end in 1967.

end the season with 44 League goals to his name, still Rangers' record tally for a season, and helped the club win the Scottish Cup against Kilmarnock, netting in the final, his career was already on a downward spiral. He netted a fur-

Europe

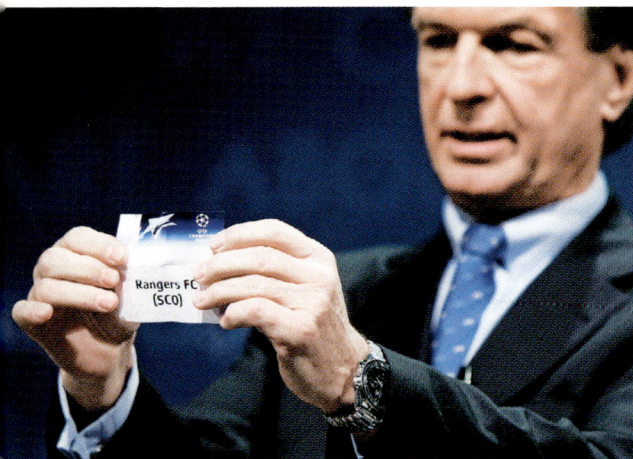

RANGERS FIRST QUALIFIED FOR the European Champions Cup (or European Cup, as it became more commonly known) in 1956-57 and have competed in the competition on 25 occasions, reaching the semi-finals in 1960. They have competed for the European Cup Winners' Cup on ten occasions, winning it once and finishing runners-up twice. The furthest they have progressed in the UEFA Cup, or its predecessor the Inter-Cities Fairs Cup is also to the semi-final stage, in 15 attempts (this figure includes those seasons where Rangers were put into the UEFA Cup after failing to make progress in the revamped UEFA Champions League).

Competition	P	W	D	L	F	A
European Cup	135	56	30	49	212	186
European Cup Winners' Cup	54	27	11	16	100	62
European Super Cup	2	0	0	2	3	6
UEFA Cup*	69	32	15	22	99	74
Total	260	115	56	89	414	328

*UEFA Cup total includes matches played in the Inter-Cities Fairs Cup.

European Cup Winners' Cup

RANGERS' FINEST EUROPEAN moments, a few European Champions Cup/UEFA Champions League matches notwithstanding, have come in the now defunct European Cup Winners' Cup. Their first tilt at the competition came in the inaugural 1960-61 season when they reached the final, which was held over two legs for the first and only time in the competition's history. Having overcome Wolverhampton Wanderers in the semi-final, Rangers were confident they could become the first British winners of a major European trophy, but particularly cynical opposition in the Italian club Fiorentina won both legs to register a 4-1 aggregate victory, with Rangers also missing a penalty in the home leg.

Six years later Rangers again made the final, disposing of West German holders Borussia Dortmund 2-1 on aggregate in the second round and winning the quarter-final against Real Zaragoza on the toss of a coin, with Rangers captain John Greig correctly

calling after the two sides had finished level at 2-2 on aggregate. Home and away victories over Slavia Sofia put Rangers into the final against the other West German entrants Bayern Munich, and with the final being held just down the road from Munich, in Nuremberg! Up against a side that could boast the talents of Sepp Maier, Franz Beckenbauer and Gerd Muller, Rangers could claim to have done well to contain their opponents to a single goal,

LEFT Rangers are drawn against Villarreal during the draw for the knock-out round of the Champions League at the UEFA headquarters, 2005

BELOW Rangers playing against Bayern Munich in the European Cup Winners Cup, May 1967

ABOVE Willie Johnston who contributed two goals in the 1971-1972 European Cup Winners' Cup final

Dinamo Moscow, with the match being played at Barcelona's Nou Camp stadium. For fifty or so minutes, everything went Rangers' way, going into a 3-0 lead thanks to goals from Willie Johnston (two) and Colin Stein, although a late Russian rally brought the match back to 3-2 some three minutes from the end. Rangers held on to register their victory, with the thousands of Rangers fans in the stadium sweeping onto the pitch in celebration. Whilst the relationship between the fans and the Spanish police had been cordial before and during the match, the police took the invasion to be something more sinister and responded by baton charging those on the field. The fans responded in kind and a battle royal ensued, with the result that the trophy and medal presentation was cancelled, with John Greig receiving the trophy in a small ante-room inside the stadium. UEFA held Rangers to be responsible and banned the club from European competition for two years, later reduced to one on appeal, although Rangers did get to play Ajax in the two-legged European Super Cup, losing both legs in a 6-3 aggregate defeat.

scored eleven minutes into extra time, but Rangers' own deficiencies up front meant they lost 1-0.

Five years later Rangers returned to the final, beating Bayern Munich in the semi-final having lost to them in the Inter-Cities Fairs Cup the previous season. Their opponents in the final were

Ferguson

THE YOUNGER BROTHER OF FORMER Rangers favourite Derek Ferguson, Barry was born in Glasgow on 2 February 1978 and was a schoolboy fan of the club, joining them as a junior at the age of 13 and being upgraded to the professional ranks in July 1994.

His first team debut came in the 3-1 defeat by Hearts in May 1997, although Rangers had already secured their ninth consecutive League title, and Barry was widely expected to be a permanent fixture in the side thereafter, his all-action midfield style being seen as vital to the team's continued success. Walter Smith had other ideas, using Barry sparingly in what turned out to be the manager's last season at Ibrox, and it was not until the arrival of Dick Advocaat that Barry featured more regularly. Indeed, Advocaat decided to build the side around Barry, with the player being made club captain

in October 2000 and helping them lift eight trophies over the next four years, including three League titles (1999, 2000 and 2003), two League Cups (2000 and 2003) and three Scottish Cups (2000, 2002 and 2003) as well as two domestic trebles and the accolade of Scottish Player of the Year in 2003.

Soon after the 2003-04 season kicked off, Barry was transferred to Blackburn Rovers for £7.5 million and the following year was appointed club captain in place of Garry Flitcroft by manager Graeme Souness. Despite the responsibility of being captain, Barry never really settled at Blackburn and in January 2005 jumped at the chance of a return to Ibrox, costing Rangers £4.5 million and helping them win the League title with a last gasp win over Hibernian. He was awarded an MBE in the 2006 Queen's Birthday Honours List for his services to football.

ABOVE Barry Ferguson – early on in his Rangers career

Formation

LIKE MANY OF TODAY'S FAMOUS football clubs Rangers had a humble beginning, being little more than a boys' club when first formed in February 1872. According to legend, brothers Peter and Moses McNeil, William McBeath and Peter Campbell were walking through West End Park in Glasgow when they observed a group of men playing football and resolved to form their own side.

It was Moses who came up with the name Rangers, having spotted it in a book about rugby, and for the next few weeks the four set about training and recruiting others to join their team. By May of that year they had secured the services of Harry and William McNeil (Peter's and Moses's brothers), John Campbell (Peter's brother) John Hunter, Willie McKinnon and Willie Miller and others long since forgotten or never identified, and played their first match. This was against Callender FC and was played at Flesher's Haugh on Glasgow Green, with the match ending as a bruising 0-0 draw.

Later that summer Rangers played their second match, an 11-0 victory over Clyde (not the present Clyde side), although no record exists of the line-up and therefore the identity of who scored Rangers' first ever goal. This is not entirely surprising, for who would have thought that what was then a youth side (no player was older than 20 years of age) would go on to become one of the most famous clubs in the world. What is known is that in this match the club wore the light blue shirt for the first time (in their opening match only four players had actually changed into something approaching football kit, the rest playing in their street clothes), and even though today's shirt is nearer to royal blue in colour, the club are still known as the Light Blues.

By the spring of the following year, 1873, Rangers had recruited further players and held their first general meeting at which various club officers were elected. A year later Rangers

became members of the Scottish Football Association and entered into the Scottish FA Cup in October 1874, beating Oxford 2-0 in the first round. They reached the final for the first time before the decade was out, in 1879, although they drew with Vale of Leven and declined to participate in the replay! Their first major trophy came in 1891 when they finished joint Champions of the Scottish League (they finished level on points with Dumbarton and the pair then drew a championship decider, prompting the decision to proclaim them joint Champions) and they have gone on to register a further 106 major trophy wins, a world record.

Gascoigne

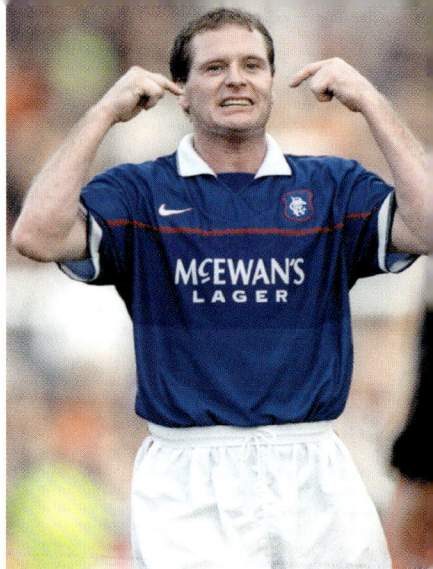

PAUL GASCOIGNE GENERATED almost as many headlines for his off-the-field capers as he did for his on-the-field accomplishments, irrespective of where he happened to be playing. Born in Gateshead on 27 May 1967, he broke into the Newcastle United side whilst still a teenager and was proclaimed as one of the brightest midfield talents to have emerged in many a year, with none other than Jackie Milburn extolling his virtues.

He was sold to Tottenham Hotspur for a then record £2 million in July 1988, subsequently breaking into the England first team and being one of the star performers in England's run to the World Cup semi-final in 1990. The following season he was in inspirational form, scoring numerous vital goals, including a stunning free kick in the semi-final against Arsenal as Spurs made it to the FA Cup Final to face Nottingham Forest. Off the field there was mounting speculation that Paul might be sold to Lazio for some £8 million to alleviate growing debts, whilst on the field the player appeared to be hyped up for such a crucial match and was guilty of two sickening challenges. The second, on Gary Charles, resulted in Paul suffering serious cruciate damage and was put out of the game for over a year.

Paul did sign for Lazio for a reduced £5.5 million in May 1992 and spent just over three years in

Italy before heading home in July 1995. He joined Rangers in a deal worth £4.3 million, seemingly still to fulfil the potential he had shown as a youngster. Whilst he was to enjoy some success at Ibrox, helping the club win the League title in 1996 and 1997, the Scottish Cup in 1996 and the League Cup in 1997, the old demons where seldom far away. An ill-advised decision to act as though playing the flute in a match against Celtic resulted in death threats from the IRA and he collected too many bookings for arguing with referees. Some of the problems were not of his making, however, for in one match he found that referee Dougie Smith had dropped his yellow card and Paul retrieved it, brandishing it in front of the astonished referee as though to reprimand him for his carelessness. The less than amused referee failed to enter into the spirit of the occasion, booking Paul Gascoigne for his impertinence.

In March 1998 Paul was sold to Middlesbrough for £3.45 million, thus bringing to an end his at times turbulent Ibrox career, but he left friends and memories by the score.

Goram

RIGHT Andy Goram on international duty

BELOW Richard Gough, Andy Goram and Stuart McCall

BORN IN BURY ON 13 APRIL 1964, goalkeeper Andy Goram began his playing career with Oldham Athletic and spent seven seasons at Boundary Park,

winning the first four of his 43 caps for Scotland whilst with the club. He joined Hibernian in 1987 but was unable to lift the Edinburgh club above mid-table mediocrity, although he continued to add to his tally of international caps.

A £1 million fee took him to Rangers

in June 1991 and he stepped straight into the first team, helping them win the League title six seasons in succession and thus complete the infamous 'nine in a row' as well as two Scottish Cups and two League Cups. Andy was one of the star performers during Rangers' European exploits in 1992-93, which saw them come within one match of reaching the final of the UEFA Champions League.

When his Rangers career came to an end he played for Motherwell, Notts County, Sheffield United, Manchester United, Coventry City, Queen of the South and Elgin City before turning to coaching, currently serving Airdrie United as goalkeeping coach. Andy was an often controversial figure owing to his supposed political allegiances and when he was diagnosed as schizophrenic, opposing fans took delight in chanting 'Two Andy Gorams, There's Only Two Andy Gorams'!

Andy was also a talented cricketer, appearing for the Scottish cricket side four times, twice against Ireland and twice in the Nat West Trophy, bowling out England Test player Richard Blakey in a NatWest Trophy match against Yorkshire in 1989.

Gough

BORN IN STOCKHOLM TO a Swedish mother and Scottish father on 5 April 1962, Richard Gough grew up in South Africa and came to Scotland in 1980 to play in a trial for Rangers. They turned him down, so Richard underwent another trial, this time with Dundee United and proved successful. Although Richard briefly returned to his then home in South Africa suffering from homesickness, he eventually returned to Dundee United and proved a worthwhile acquisition, helping them win the Scottish League in 1983 against all odds.

Richard was to spend six seasons with Dundee United and by 1986 a number of bigger clubs were clamouring for his signature. Although Rangers were believed to have offered £900,000 for him, Dundee

United would not sell him to another Scottish club and so he went to Spurs for £750,000. He was to spend a little over a year at White Hart Lane, helping the club reach the FA Cup Final in 1987, but by December 1987 he was homesick again and looking for a return to Scotland. This time Rangers got their man, Graeme Souness paying £1.1 million to bring him to Ibrox, better late than never!

Made captain he would go on to lead the club to the nine consecutive League titles, forming a particularly effective club partnership with Terry Butcher. Unfortunately, Scotland did not possess another centre-back with the abilities of either Gough or Butcher and after a particular hammering, Richard fell out with the national manager Andy Roxburgh having made 61 appearances for his chosen country (he was qualified to play for Sweden, South Africa or Scotland and chose Scotland) and was never selected again, with Roxburgh's successor Craig Brown also choosing to overlook a player who was undoubtedly the best central-back available to the country.

Richard remained at Ibrox until 1997 when he joined Kansas City Wizards in the United States Major League, subsequently going on to play for San Jose Clash. Richard's playing career came to an end with spells at Everton (where he was reunited with former Rangers manager Walter Smith) and Nottingham Forest and he eventually returned to Scotland in November 2004 to take over as manager of Livingston. Although he saved the club from relegation from the Premier League, he resigned in May 2005 and returned to America for family reasons.

BELOW Gough in action

Greatest XI

A VOTE AMONGST THOUSANDS OF
Rangers fans for their greatest ever team
was held in 1999 and resulted in the following eleven players being selected:

1	Andy Goram
2	John Greig
3	Sandy Jardine
4	Richard Gough
5	Terry Butcher
6	Jim Baxter
7	Davie Cooper
8	Paul Gascoigne
9	Ally McCoist
10	Mark Hateley
11	Brian Laudrup

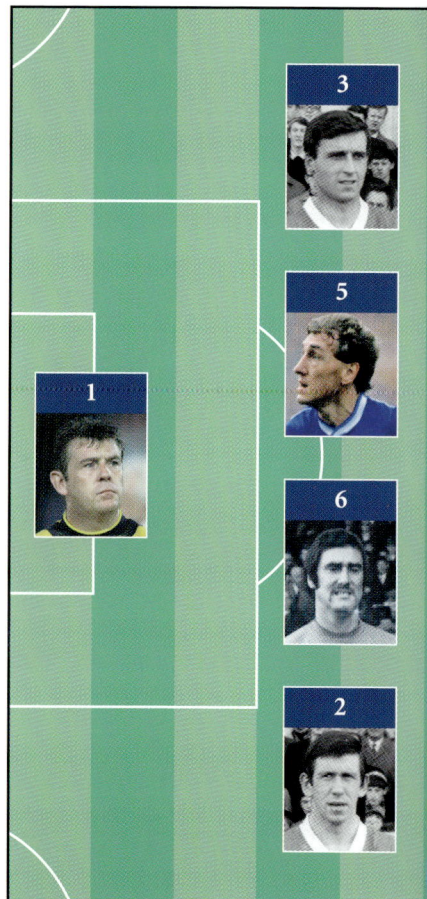

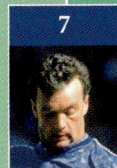

Greig

ONE OF THE FINEST SERVANTS THE club has ever had, John Greig was born in Edinburgh on 11 September 1942 and grew up a Heart of Midlothian fan! Despite this, he has served only one club throughout his career, Rangers, and is regarded by many both inside and outside the club as the Greatest Ever Ranger, an accolade he was awarded after a 1999 vote among supporters.

He scored on what was his first team debut, against Airdrie in a League Cup match in 1961 and would go on to register 857 appearances for the first team, including 498 in League matches alone. His time as a player saw him collect five League titles, six Scottish Cups and four League Cups, figures that include three domestic doubles, in 1964, 1976 and 1978. Perhaps his finest moment came in 1972, when he collected the European Cup Winners' Cup, although the event was overshadowed by rioting on the pitch by Rangers supporters and the cup was actually collected out of sight in the dressing room after the match.

Whilst his worth to Rangers was never questioned, he was equally vital to the Scottish national side, winning 44 caps for his country between 1964 and 1971 and captaining the side for three years. At the end of his playing career, which saw him named Player of the Year twice, he was awarded a testimonial by Rangers that drew a crowd of 65,000 for a match against Scotland at Ibrox, with John scoring twice in the 5-0 win.

Following his retirement he turned to management, taking over from Jock Wallace and bringing further Scottish Cup and League Cup success, although the League title itself proved elusive. Although his time as manager was not as successful as many had hoped, he was responsible for bringing in many great Rangers players, including Ally McCoist, Derek Ferguson and Robert Fleck. He resigned in 1983 to be replaced by the returning Jock Wallace, going into broadcasting and travel management but still a regular sight around Ibrox. In January 1990 he returned to Rangers on a more permanent basis, being appointed director of public relations. Early in 2004 he was appointed to the board of directors at Rangers.

BELOW John Greig in the 1967 team photo

Hamilton

BORN IN ELGIN IN 1877, ROBERT Cumming Hamilton, known within the club as RC, was perhaps the club's most prolific goalscorer in the period from its formation to the First World War, when his playing career effectively came to an end. Whilst many of the records he set during his heyday have since been beaten, there is one record he still retains, that of scoring more goals against Celtic than any other Rangers player.

RC had graduate from Glasgow University and would eventually become a schoolmaster, but he also excelled at football, playing for Elgin City and Queen's Park before joining Rangers in 1897. In his first season with the club he scored 18 goals in 15 League matches and bettered that a year later with 21 in 18 as Rangers won the League without dropping a point.

He also scored four goals in the club's run to the Scottish Cup final to give him a tally of 25 goals; had the European Boot for the top goalscorer been in existence then RC would have won it, a feat he repeated in 1903-04 with 28 goals in all competitions.

In all he won five League titles and two Scottish Cups as well as 11 caps for Scotland and would also play for Fulham, Morton, Hearts and Dundee during his career. He also worked at the family net manufacturing business before his death in 1948.

ABOVE Ibrox Stadium the home of Rangers

Hateley

THE SON OF FORMER FOOTBALLER Tony Hateley (Chelsea, Liverpool and Aston Villa, among others), Mark was born in Liverpool on 7 November 1961 and began his professional career with Coventry City, another of his father's former clubs, and would go on to make more than 100 appearances for the Sky Blues.

He joined Portsmouth for £220,000 in 1983 and made an immediate impact, scoring 22 League goals in just 32 appearances and was rewarded with his first cap for England. Whilst many of England's bigger sides cast envious eyes at Mark, it was AC Milan of Italy that stepped in with a £915,000 offer in 1984.

Nicknamed Attila by the AC Milan fans, he proved immensely popular and effective and would spend four years with the club. He then joined AS Monaco and helped them win the French League title before a further £1 million move to Rangers in the summer of 1990. Whilst he had enjoyed considerable success prior to his move to Ibrox, it was his time at Rangers that proved most rewarding. Five League titles, two Scottish Cups and three League Cups tell the story in bare statistics, but Mark's exploits in the Light Blue shirt were more the stuff of 'Roy of the Rovers' – his two goals against Aberdeen in the final match of the 1990-91 season snatched the title away from their opponents in dramatic fashion.

In November 1995 he joined the other Rangers, Queens Park Rangers of London in a £1.5 million deal but struggled to win over the fans, prompting a loan move to Leeds United. They knew all about his abilities, having been on the receiving end of a thunderbolt goal in the European Champions League in 1991. In March 1997 Mark sensationally returned to Ibrox to help out a side decimated by injury and helped them win the title again, the key result being a 1-0 win over Celtic that saw Mark sent off but do enough whilst on the

field to put Celtic off their stride. The three wins Rangers recorded with Mark in the side that season enabled them to finish five points ahead of Celtic at the end of the campaign.

Released on a free transfer, Mark then took over as player-manager of Hull City and when his playing career came to an end turned to doing commentary work for Setanta Sports.

Honours

RANGERS HAVE WON AN ASTON-ishing 107 major trophies in their long and illustrious history, being the first club in the world to win 50 League titles and the first to register 100 major trophies. For the purposes of this table, the tally also includes victories in the Glasgow Cup, for many years an important part of the Scottish football fixture list, especially as it often pitted Rangers against Celtic.

Scottish League Champions

1891* 1899 1900 1901 1902 1911 1912
1913 1918 1920 1921 1923 1924 1925
1927 1928 1929 1930 1931 1933 1934
1935 1937 1939 1947 1949 1950 1953
1956 1957 1959 1961 1963 1964 1975
1976 1978 1987 1989 1990 1991 1992
1993 1994 1995 1996 1997 1999 2000
2003 2005 *Joint champions

Scottish FA Cup winners

1894 1897 1898 1903 1928 1930 1932
1934 1935 1936 1948 1949 1950 1953
1960 1962 1963 1964 1966 1973 1976
1978 1979 1981 1992 1993 1996 1999
2000 2002 2003

Scottish League Cup winners

1946 1948 1960 1961 1963 1964 1970
1975 1977 1978 1981 1983 1984 1986
1987 1988 1990 1992 1993 1996 1998
2002 2003 2005

European Cup Winners' Cup winners

1972

Glasgow Cup

1893 1894 1897 1898 1900 1901 1902
1911 1912 1913 1914 1918 1919 1922
1923 1924 1925 1930 1932 1933 1934
1936 1937 1938 1940 1942 1943 1944
1945 1948 1950 1954 1957 1958 1960
1969 1971 1975* 1976 1979 1983 1985
1986 1987 *Trophy shared

Glasgow Merchants and Charity Cup

1879 1897 1900 1904 1906 1907 1909
1911 1919 1922 1923 1925 1928 1929
1930 1931 1932 1933 1934 1939 1940
1941 1942 1944 1945 1946 1947 1948
1951 1955 1957 1960

ABOVE Celebrations after winning the Skol Cup in 1986

Ibrox

THE BOYS' CLUB THAT THE McNeil brothers Peter and Moses helped form in 1872 played their first matches on Glasgow Green, with Peter McNeil often having to arrive at the chosen venue extremely early in order to ensure the pitch was marked and ready and, more importantly, not taken by another team! Such was the way of football in the nineteenth century, with the arrangement of a fixture no guarantee that the match would take place, especially if another club, with bigger and older boys, had taken a shine to the carefully marked pitch.

It was Queen's Park's refusal to meet Rangers in a friendly as they had no pitch of their own that prompted the decision to search for their own enclosure. The first of these was found at Burnbank in 1875, near Kelvin Bridge, a ground that

was sufficiently close to where many of the then players lived, and was formally opened with a fixture against Vale of Leven, then probably the second most famous club in the land, with Rangers drawing the historic fixture 1-1 on 11 September 1875.

Less than a year later, in August 1876, Rangers left Burnbank for Kinning Park, a ground that had previously been home to Clydesdale (the previous occupants moved to Titwood, where they remain as

a cricket club) and a month later Vale of Leven again provided the opposition, winning 2-1 on 2 September 1876.

Kinning Park was to remain Rangers' ground for the next ten years, increasing the capacity from 2,000 (a crowd of 1,500 witnessed the opening match against Vale of Leven) to 7,000 and making numerous improvements to both the pitch and facilities for spectators, although this ground was leased and by 1884 there came rumours that the landlords would eventually like the site back for other development. In the event Rangers held on to it until February 1887, finishing the season at Cathkin Park but having already secured another property a few miles west of Kinning Park.

The pitch was surrounded by a running track, with a grandstand capable of seating 1,200 built along one side, and a pavilion, with changing rooms, bathrooms and offices, was constructed in one corner. The first Ibrox Park was officially opened with a friendly match against Preston North End on 20 August 1887, with the 'Invincibles' winning 8-1 when the match was abandoned after

some 70 minutes when the crowd, which numbered some 15,000 spilled out onto the field.

Rangers outgrew this home too and so began work on an adjacent site on an even grander scale. A two storey pavilion was built in the south-east corner, together with a grandstand, with the roof taken from the previous Ibrox ground, provided seating and cover for 4,500. The new Ibrox Park comprised some 14.5 acres of land and could, claimed the club, hold 80,000 spectators, although 75,000 would be nearer the mark.

It was this capacity figure that led to Ibrox being chosen to host the Scotland and England fixture in April 1902, but a significant part of the crowd was to be accommodated on wooden terracing, which in turn was on an iron framework, hardly the safest of environments. So it proved, for midway through the match seven rows of terracing just simply collapsed, sending hundreds down into the void that had been created. Twenty-five died and a further 587 were injured, many seriously. The wooden terracing was subsequently removed, reducing Ibrox's capacity to 25,000 in 1905.

Extensive work done by Archibald Leitch, the pre-eminent football ground designer, saw the construction of a massive grandstand, which would seat 10,500 and hold thousands more standing in the enclosure, the undoubted focal point of a ground that was elliptical in shape. Ibrox's capacity grew and grew, from 60,000 in 1905 to 80,000 after the First World War and beyond 100,000 by the time of the Second World War, with more than 118,000 packing in for the fixture against Celtic on 1 January 1939.

Although much work went into getting as many spectators into the ground as was possible, little or no thought appeared to be given to how they would leave the ground after matches. Fans turn up for matches over a number of hours but try to leave in a matter of minutes as soon as the game is over, a major factor in the events of another New Year's clash with Celtic, this one in 1971. Stairway 13 had proved a hazard for much of the stadium's history, with numerous incidents prior to 1971, but it was this 1-1 draw that was to see one of the worst disasters in British sporting history, with 66 spectators dead from traumatic asphyxiation after someone was believed to have tripped over at the top of the stairway.

Over the next ten years, Ibrox changed out of all recognition, with the elliptical shape disappearing and a rectangular ground arising in its place. The Archibald Leitch stand remains, an almost constant reminder of Ibrox's former glories, but three brand new stands, almost identical in design and construction, gave the ground a capacity of just over 46,000. Later work in filling in the corners, creating an enclosed stadium with a capacity of 51,000, turned Ibrox into one of the most impressive stadiums in the world.

ABOVE A section of the terracing which collapsed at Ibrox Park

ing outside the stadium and burning their scarves and season tickets as Rangers knowingly signed a Catholic for the first time. Even Mo Johnston acknowledged the situation he now found himself in, claiming that he had managed to unite Glasgow, for now both Rangers and Celtic fans hated him! To further add to his woes, UEFA fined him £3,500 for 'unsporting conduct' for reneging on his return to Celtic Park!

A tally of 51 goals in 110 appearances for Rangers no doubt went some way to placate the Rangers faction that had been most vociferous against his arrival (though quite what it did for Celtic fans has never been revealed!) and perhaps paved the way for other Catholics who have since signed for the club.

Mo remained at Ibrox until 1991 when he left to join Everton in a £1.5 million deal. He later returned to Scotland, with significantly less fanfare, to play for Hearts and Falkirk. He finished his playing career in America with Kansas City Wizards and later became coach and then manager to the MetroStars, a team that later became re-branded as Red Bull New York.

Johnstone

BORN IN DUNDEE ON 4 NOVEMBER 1953, Derek Johnstone was a schoolboy fan of Dundee United and trained with the club as a youngster but subsequently joined Rangers as a schoolboy in December 1968, being upgraded to the professional ranks in July 1970.

That same year he ensured his place in the record books, earning a place in the League Cup Final side to face Celtic whilst still ten days short of his seventeenth birthday and headed home the only goal of the game to secure the trophy. That was to be the first of many he won whilst with the club, collecting a total of three League titles, the

Scottish Cup five times and the League Cup five times as well as a winners' medal from the European Cup Winners' Cup in 1972. Whilst he favoured playing at centre-half, such

was his versatility he also slotted in at centre-forward and in the midfield, performing in all three areas for both club and country and going on to win 14 caps for Scotland.

Derek remained at Ibrox until 1983 when he was sold to Chelsea for £30,000, but struggled to command a regular place in the side, prompting a loan move to Dundee United and then an eventual return to Ibrox. His second stint at the club was not as successful as his first and he left the club for good in 1986 and after a brief spell as player-manager of Partick Thistle left the game in order to pursue a media career. In all Derek hit 209 goals in 547 first team appearances for Rangers, one of the best post war records.

Klos

BORN IN DORTMUND ON 16 AUGUST 1971, Stefan Klos began his professional career with his local side Borussia Dortmund in 1991, going on to help them win the UEFA Champions League in 1997 with a 3-1 win over Juventus. Despite this victory, Stefan was soon at odds with the German club over his contract and was eventually allowed to leave in December 1998, joining Rangers for £700,000.

He soon proved the ideal long-term replacement for Andy Goram, helping the club win the League and Scottish Cup at the end of the season. He has since gone on to add a further three League titles, three Scottish Cups and two League Cups, proving to be a resounding success as the last line of defence. Although overlooked at international level, his worth to Rangers has always been appreciated, being appointed captain in the summer of 2004.

He picked up a cruciate ligament injury the following January that was to sideline him for the rest of the season and even though Stefan recovered by the start of the 2005-06 campaign, he faced stiff competition from Ronald Waterreus for the goalkeeping berth at Rangers.

ABOVE Stefan Klos organises his defence

LEFT Derek Johnstone

Laudrup

RIGHT Brian Laudrup
in action

THE YOUNGER BROTHER of the equally famous Michael Laudrup, Brian was born in Vienna, Austria on 22 February 1969, the son of former Danish international Finn Laudrup. Brian began his playing career with Brondby and earned his first international cap aged just 18 in the 1-0 defeat by West Germany in November 1987.

Although not selected for the Danish squad for the 1988 European Championships he became a regular in the side the following year and earned a big money move to Uerdingen for £650,000 having been named Danish Player of the Year. The following season he was sold to Bayern Munich for £2 million and would go on to enhance his reputation, helping Denmark win the 1992 European Championships after they were drafted in as late replacements for Yugoslavia.

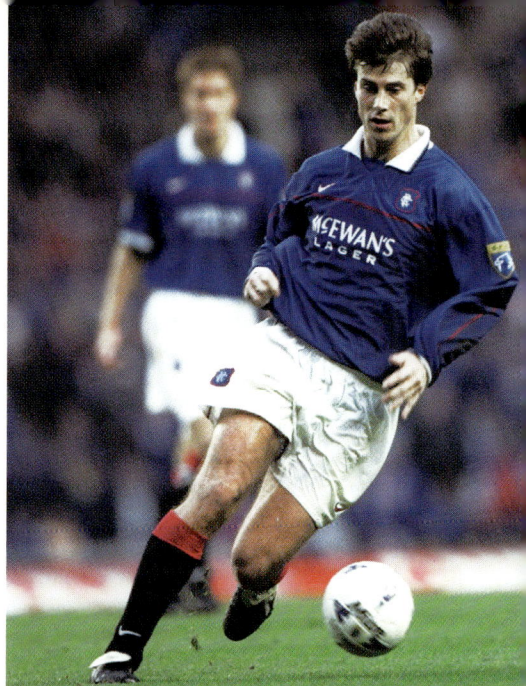

Brian then had a spell in Italy with Fiorentina and then AC Milan on loan, but his time in Italy was not a success, also hindering his international career as Denmark failed to qualify for the 1994 World Cup. In July 1994 he was sold to Rangers for £2.3 million and set about restoring his reputation as one of the most exciting players in the game, able to

ABOVE Brian Laudrup celebrates the second goal during a Scottish Premier League match against Aberdeen, 1996

both create and finish chances with equal aplomb.

His time at Ibrox brought success in the form of three League titles, the Scottish Cup and the League Cup victories, although by 1997 he was the subject of several bids from other clubs, with Ajax believed to have made a £5 million offer for his signature. Brian decided to sit tight and see out his contract, which had another year to run and then move on, eventually joining Chelsea. Expectation was not matched by accomplishment however, and he moved on to FC Copenhagen and then Ajax before injury forced him to retire at the age of 31.

Brian then turned to the media, becoming a Danish commentator for the UEFA Champions League for Danish TV as well as setting up a youth football camp with former Danish goalkeeper Lars Hogh and playing for Old Boys side Lyngby Boldklub.

League Positions

SEASON ENDING	POS	P	W	D	L	F	A	P
1891	Joint 1st	18	13	3	2	58	25	29
1892	5th	22	11	2	9	59	46	24
1893	2nd	18	12	4	2	41	27	28
1894	4th	18	8	4	6	44	30	20
1895	3rd	18	10	2	6	41	26	22
1896	2nd	18	11	4	3	57	39	26
1897	3rd	18	11	3	4	66	30	25
1898	2nd	18	13	3	2	71	15	29
1899	1st	18	18	0	0	79	18	36
1900	1st	18	15	2	1	69	27	32
1901	1st	20	17	1	2	60	25	35
1902	1st	18	13	2	3	43	29	28
1903	3rd	22	12	5	5	56	30	29
1904	4th	26	16	6	4	80	33	38
1905	2nd	26	19	3	4	83	28	41
1906	4th	30	15	7	8	58	48	37
1907	3rd	34	19	7	8	69	33	45
1908	3rd	34	21	8	5	74	40	50
1909	4th	34	19	7	8	91	38	45
1910	3rd	34	20	6	8	70	35	46
1911	1st	34	23	6	5	90	27	52
1912	1st	34	24	3	7	86	34	51
1913	1st	34	24	5	5	76	41	53
1914	2nd	38	27	5	6	79	31	59
1915	3rd	38	23	4	11	74	47	50

SEASON ENDING	POS	P	W	D	L	F	A	P
1916	2nd	38	25	6	7	87	39	56
1917	3rd	38	24	5	9	68	32	53
1918	1st	34	25	6	3	66	24	56
1919	2nd	34	26	5	3	86	16	57
1920	1st	42	31	9	2	106	25	71
1921	1st	42	35	6	1	91	24	76
1922	2nd	42	28	10	4	83	26	66
1923	1st	38	23	9	6	67	29	55
1924	1st	38	25	9	4	72	22	59
1925	1st	38	25	10	3	76	26	60
1926	6th	38	19	6	13	79	55	44
1927	1st	38	23	10	5	85	41	56
1928	1st	38	26	8	4	109	36	60
1929	1st	38	30	7	1	107	32	67
1930	1st	38	28	4	6	94	32	60
1931	1st	38	27	6	5	96	29	60
1932	2nd	38	28	5	5	118	42	61
1933	1st	38	26	10	2	113	43	62
1934	1st	38	30	6	2	118	41	66
1935	1st	38	25	5	8	96	46	55
1936	2nd	38	27	7	4	110	43	61
1937	1st	38	26	9	3	88	32	61
1938	3rd	38	18	13	7	75	49	49
1939	1st	38	25	9	4	112	55	59
1947	1st	30	21	4	5	76	26	46
1948	2nd	30	21	4	5	64	28	46
1949	1st	30	20	6	4	63	32	46
1950	1st	30	22	6	2	58	26	50
1951	2nd	30	17	4	9	64	37	38
1952	2nd	30	16	9	5	61	31	41

LEAGUE POSITIONS

SEASON ENDING	POS	P	W	D	L	F	A	P
1953	1st	30	18	7	5	80	29	43
1954	4th	30	13	8	9	56	35	34
1955	3rd	30	19	8	1	67	33	41
1956	1st	34	22	8	4	85	27	52
1957	1st	34	26	3	5	96	48	55
1958	2nd	34	22	5	7	89	49	49
1959	1st	34	21	8	5	92	51	50
1960	3rd	34	17	8	9	72	38	42
1961	1st	34	23	5	6	88	46	51
1962	2nd	34	22	7	5	84	31	51
1963	1st	34	25	7	2	94	28	57
1964	1st	34	25	5	4	85	31	55
1965	5th	34	18	8	8	78	35	44
1966	2nd	34	25	5	4	91	29	55
1967	2nd	34	24	7	3	92	29	55
1968	2nd	34	28	5	1	93	34	61
1969	2nd	34	22	7	6	81	32	49
1970	2nd	34	19	7	8	67	40	45
1971	4th	34	16	9	9	58	34	41
1972	3rd	34	21	2	11	71	38	44
1973	2nd	34	26	4	4	74	30	56
1974	3rd	34	21	6	7	67	34	48
1975	1st	34	25	6	3	86	33	56
1976	1st	36	23	8	5	60	24	54
1977	2nd	36	18	10	8	62	37	46
1978	1st	36	24	7	5	76	39	55
1979	2nd	36	18	9	9	52	35	45
1980	5th	36	15	7	14	50	46	37
1981	3rd	36	16	12	8	60	32	44
1982	3rd	36	16	11	9	57	45	43

SEASON ENDING	POS	P	W	D	L	F	A	P
1983	4th	36	13	12	11	52	41	38
1984	4th	36	15	12	9	53	41	42
1985	4th	36	13	12	11	47	38	38
1986	5th	36	13	9	14	53	45	35
1987	1st	44	31	7	6	85	23	69
1988	3rd	44	26	8	10	85	34	60
1989	1st	36	26	4	6	62	26	56
1990	1st	36	20	11	5	48	19	51
1991	1st	36	24	7	5	62	23	55
1992	1st	44	33	6	5	101	31	72
1993	1st	44	33	7	4	97	35	73
1994	1st	44	22	14	8	74	41	58
1995	1st	36	20	9	7	60	35	69
1996	1st	36	27	6	3	85	25	87
1997	1st	36	25	5	6	85	33	80
1998	2nd	36	21	9	6	76	38	72
1999	1st	36	23	8	5	78	31	77
2000	1st	36	28	6	2	96	26	90
2001	2nd	38	26	4	8	76	36	82
2002	2nd	38	25	10	3	82	27	85
2003	1st	38	31	4	3	101	28	97
2004	2nd	38	31	5	2	105	25	98
2005	1st	38	29	6	3	78	22	93
2006	3rd	38	21	10	7	67	37	73

Manager

DESPITE BEING FORMED MORE than 130 years ago, only eleven different men have managed Rangers prior to Paul Le Guen's arrival in 2006. The first of these, William Wilton, served the club as a player from 1883, was elected a member of the committee that supervised the move from Kinning Park to Ibrox in 1887, became match secretary in 1889 and was appointed manager ten years later when the club became a limited company. Here are those who have managed the club through their long and illustrious history.

McCoist

GENERALLY CONSIDERED ONE OF the greatest goalscorers in Rangers' history, Ally McCoist actually turned the club down twice before finally arriving at Ibrox! Born in Bellshill on 24 September 1962, his first opportunity at joining the club came as a schoolboy, but he declined the offer in order to sign for St Johnstone, subsequently turning professional with them in December 1978. After making four appearances in 1978-79 and 15 the following season, all without scoring, Ally burst onto the scene with 22 goals in 38 appearances during the 1980-81 season.

Such goalscoring exploits attracted considerable attention from other clubs, with Rangers among those willing to pay what it took to get him to Ibrox, but Ally opted for a move south of the border to Sunderland, signing in a deal worth £400,000, then a huge sum for a player still in his teens. Defences in England proved harder to break down, with Ally scoring just 8 goals in his 56 appearances for the Roker Park club and desperate to return to Scotland, Rangers finally got their man at the third time of asking, paying £185,000 in June 1983.

His first season at Ibrox was hardly a return to former glories either, netting nine goals in 30 appearances, prompting speculation that he might be on his

BELOW Ally McCoist wins the ball in this challenge

travels once again, but Ally got down to some hard work and by 1984-85 the goals began to flow with regularity. Indeed, by the time his Ibrox career came to an end, Ally had hit the net on no fewer than 251 occasions in League matches, a Rangers record, and 355 times in all competitions, ensuring that he holds the goalscoring record for League, the League Cup and Europe. Such goalscoring helped Rangers win ten League titles, the League Cup on nine occasions and the

Scottish Cup once (his medal haul in this competition might have been higher had he not suffered from injuries at the wrong times), whilst on a personal level he was the European Golden Boot winner in 1992 and 1993 and named Player of the Year in 1992. His tally of goals also included an astonishing 28 hat tricks, another club record.

Whilst his goalscoring exploits at club level proved hard to reproduce at international level, he is still the fifth highest scorer in Scotland's history with 19 goals in his 61 matches for his country. Sixty of these caps came whilst on Rangers' books, the other came after he had left the club for Kilmarnock and was supposedly in the twilight of his career. At the end of his playing career Ally turned to coaching, linking up with former club manager Walter Smith with the national squad and a career in the media, having been one of the captains on A Question of Sport.

ABOVE Ally McCoist celebrates with the trophy after the Skol Cup final victory against Aberdeen, 1987

MIDDLE Ally McCoist shoots during the Scottish Cup Final match against Celtic, 1989

OPPOSITE Ally McCoist of Rangers in action, 1995

McNeill

RIGHT Moses McNeill would have been proud of Ibrox

EVEN IF MOSES MCNEIL had achieved little or nothing of note on the field he would still be assured a place in the club's history, for he was one of the original founding fathers who took a stroll through West End Park in Glasgow and came up with the idea of forming a football club. It was also Moses who came up with the name Rangers, spotting it in a book about an English rugby club and believed it to be the perfect name for their new football club.

Moses was born in Rhu on 29 October 1855 and was one of seven brothers, of whom four were to go on to play for Rangers, with Moses being joined by Peter, Harry and William. Only James, John and Alec never played for the club, but they would certainly have taken an interest in the exploits of their younger brothers, especially when Moses went on to become the first Rangers player to earn international honours, appearing in Scotland's 4-0 win over Wales in Glasgow in March 1876. Four years later Moses earned his second and final cap for his country, a 4-5 defeat in Glasgow at the hands of England.

Tough tackling and tricky as a winger, Moses was to also appear in two Scottish Cup finals for Rangers, both against Vale of Leven, losing after a replay in 1877 and finishing level in 1879 – Rangers refused to play in the replay and lost by default! Thereafter his appearances for the club became sporadic, with his latest coming in a friendly against Aston Villa in March 1882. Thereafter he concentrated on his profession as a commercial traveller and died in 1938.

McPhail

BOB MCPHAIL WAS BORN IN Barrhead and first came to prominence with Airdrie, helping them win the Scottish Cup in 1924 whilst aged just 18. It was to begin a love affair with the competition for Bob, for he went on to collect a further six winners' medals.

His performances for Airdrie, displaying a coolness in front of goal that belied his tender years did not go unnoticed by Rangers and in 1927 they paid £5,000, then a considerable fee, to bring him to Ibrox. He was to form an uncanny partnership with Alan Morton and later Davie Kinnear on the left wing, but it was his ability to gel with fellow strikers Sam English and Jimmy Smith that proved most beneficial to the club. Bob was to score a total of 230 League goals for the club, a record figure that was to survive nearly sixty years before being overtaken by Ally McCoist, having previously scored 70 for Airdrie.

Aside from his seven Scottish Cup medals, Bob was also to collect nine League titles and 17 caps for Scotland, scoring seven goals. The outbreak of the Second World War effectively brought his Rangers career to an end, although he did make a number of wartime appearances for both Rangers (adding a further three goals to his tally) and St Mirren before retiring in 1941. He later had a spell as reserve team trainer at Ibrox.

BELOW Bob McPhail

Meiklejohn

THE GREATEST EVER RANGERS Team, announced in 1999, omitted the name of Davie Meiklejohn, as it did many of his contemporaries, simply because those who voted on the list had not seen Davie play. If they had they would have marvelled at his performances at both right-half and centre-half, as sure and commanding a centre-back as ever turned out for the club. They would also have seen a captain who ranks alongside the most inspirational the club ever had, a motivating driving force behind an unquenchable thirst for honours.

Davie was born in Govan in 1900 and joined Rangers from Maryhill Juniors and made his debut in the 2-0 win over Aberdeen in March 1920, going on to help the club win the League title at the end of the season having made ten appearances and scored two goals. It was to be the first of no fewer than twelve League titles won whilst at Ibrox over the next sixteen years, and for good measure Davie also collected five winners' medals in the Scottish Cup, scoring one of Rangers' goals from the penalty spot in the 4-0 win against Celtic in 1928 having lost on his two previous final appearances.

Davie also won 15 caps for Scotland, captaining the side twice, and was respected throughout the game. He also received considerable credit from all sections of the media for his actions in

ABOVE Rangers captain Davie Meiklejohn (right) shakes hands with the captain of one of the 14 North American sides that Rangers met during their tour, 1930

the infamous clash with Celtic in 1931 when Celtic goalkeeper John Thomson was accidentally killed diving at the feet of Sam English; it was Davie who recognised the seriousness of the situation, beckoning the medical staff to attend to the stricken player and silencing a section of the Rangers crowd who had begun barracking the fallen player.

He remained a Rangers player until 1936 when he retired from playing and went to work for the newspaper The Daily Record. Davie was lured back to football after the war, becoming Partick Thistle manager in 1947. He collapsed and died on 22 August 1959 whilst in the directors' box at Broomfield.

Morton

ALAN MORTON GAVE RANGERS more than fifty years of service and is rightly regarded as one of the most important men who walked through the doors of Ibrox. Indeed, visitors to Ibrox can see for themselves the esteem with which he is held, even today, for a portrait of Alan in his football strip stands at the top of the marble staircase in the Main Stand.

Born in Glasgow in 1893, he began his career with Queen's Park, the famous amateur side, and was targeted by Rangers by new manager Bill Struth as his first signing after taking over in 1920 when left-winger Dr Jim Paterson announced he was heading to London to pursue a medical career. Alan was persuaded to turn professional (albeit on a part-time basis) and join Rangers, making his debut against Airdrie in August 1920. By a strange quirk of fate, Alan's final appearance in a Rangers shirt was also against Airdrie, in January 1933.

In between times Alan had made 495 first team appearances, of which 382 were in the League and scored 166 goals (115 in the League alone). It was his abilities to create chances for others, however, which earned him the everlasting affection of both Rangers and Scotland followers, most notably in the infamous 1928 clash between England and Scotland at Wembley. Whilst Scotland may have started the match underdogs and under-rated, they finished with a sparkling 5-1 win, with Alan providing three crosses for Huddersfield's Alec Jackson to convert. During the match an English fan described him as a 'wee blue devil' and the nickname was applied to Alan thereafter.

Winner of nine League championship medals Alan won only one Scottish Cup winners' medal, in 1930, but this came

after the heartbreak of defeat in 1921, 1922 and 1929. Twenty-nine of his 31 caps came whilst associated with Rangers and he also represented the Scottish League on 15 occasions.

Alan combined his playing career with being a mining engineer, a profession he maintained for most of his life. When the end came to his playing career in 1933, he did not sever all links with Rangers, being appointed to the board of directors and continued to serve the club in this capacity until his death in 1971. His impact on the game, already legendary for his exploits on the field, was permanently assured thanks to his contributions as a sports administrator off it.

Negri

WHEN MARCO NEGRI ARRIVED at Ibrox in the summer of 1997 for £3.5 million from Perugia, he was seen as the obvious replacement for an ageing Ally McCoist. Marco certainly started in blistering form, setting a new Scottish Premier League record of netting in ten consecutive matches, with his tally including a haul of five against Dundee United and four against Dunfermline Athletic.

Marco (born in Milan on 27 October 1970) ended his first season at Rangers with 33 League goals in 28 appearances, although it wasn't enough to win the title, which went to Celtic. He also scored only one goal in the Scottish Cup, which went to Hearts, and none at all in the League Cup, also won by Celtic.

Despite his goals, Marco appeared to be a complex character, preferring to celebrate his numerous goals with a simple handshake. This was no show of simple modesty but rather a further example of the aloofness he carried like a torch – he did not socialise with the players away from the game and seemingly had no friends in it. Then he picked up a serious eye injury whilst playing squash and sat out the entire 1998-99 season. He finally re-appeared in the side in May 2000, coming on as a substitute in the match at home to

Hearts, only to disappear again until October 2000 when he started against Dundee United and had a goal disallowed for offside.

According to some sources, he was picking up a colossal £18,000 a week whilst sitting around doing nothing, with successive managers Walter Smith and Dick Advocaat being unable to convince him to return to the side and actually earn his money. A proposed loan deal to Vicenza fell through before he was finally offloaded to Bologna in February 2001. His lack of commitment to the game that gave him a great living wasn't confined to Rangers either, for he made just two substitute appearances in two years back home in Italy before dropping down into Serie B with Livorno. He later had a trial at Derby County – Rangers fans remain convinced he should have had one in Glasgow to explain what went wrong!

Numan

BORN IN HEEMSKERK ON 14 December 1969, Arthur Numan was Rangers manager Dick Advocaat's first signing when taking over at Ibrox in 1998, Advocaat returning to his former club PSV Eindhoven to pay £4.5 million for a player who had established a reputation as one of the best full-backs in the Dutch game.

Arthur began his career with amateur club SV Beverwijk before being spotted by Haarlemm, where coach Dick Advocaat switched him from an attacking midfield player to a more defensive full-back. It was this switch that turned him into one of the best defenders in the Dutch game, prompting a move to FC Twente in 1991.

Made captain of the club Arthur also skippered the Dutch Under-21 side before earning a big money move to PSV Eindhoven. In October 1992 he was awarded his first full cap for his country, where Dick Advocaat was coach, although he was substituted after just 25 minutes in the match against Poland. By the time the curtain came down on his international career, he had 45 caps to his name and had helped Holland finish fourth in the 1998 World Cup.

That summer he joined Rangers, following his former manager and coach Dick Advocaat to Ibrox. The season started promisingly enough, with victory in the League Cup over St Johnstone, but although the League title was won, Arthur made only eight appearances during the course of the season owing to injury. He returned the following campaign, which saw the League and Scottish Cup double success and was the captain that lifted the trophy after Aberdeen had been beaten in the Scottish Cup final.

Arthur was to collect a further five winners' medals during his time at

Ibrox, with double cup success in 2001-02 being followed by a domestic clean sweep the following term. This proved to be the final season for Arthur, who announced his retirement from playing at the end of the season. Despite overtures from Villarreal of Spain, Arthur remained true to his word, preferring to pursue a new career in the media.

ABOVE Ricksen, Ronald de Boer, Arveladze, Numan and Mols celebrate after winning the Tennents Scottish Cup final in 2003

Oddities

WHILST RANGERS HAVE lifted the Scottish Cup on no fewer than 31 occasions, they came mightily close to winning the English FA Cup, reaching the semi-final stage in 1887!

Rangers had already beaten Everton, Church, Cowlairs, Lincoln City and Old Westminsters on their way to the semi-final, where they would face Aston Villa at Nantwich Road in Crewe. The route to the Aston Villa tie had not been without some controversy, for in the middle of the night before their tie against Everton, the entire Rangers side had been ejected from their Liverpool hotel after the proprietor had objected to the noise and revelry! Despite this, Rangers had gone on to beat Everton 1-0.

According to legend, before the Aston Villa clash the Rangers team were entertained by their former player Hugh McIntyre, who provided some of the players with a meal on the morning of the match. The Rangers goalkeeper Willie Chalmers was said to have eaten too much and was not quite as mobile as expected during the match, which Aston Villa won 3-1 on their way to winning the FA Cup for the first time in their history.

Old Firm

RANGERS AGAINST CELTIC IS THE most intense rivalry in the world, despite the claims of other pretenders. Irrespective of the fortunes or form of either protagonist, this is the match that either side has to win in order to satisfy their fans. Whilst the fixture was seen as a straight battle between Protestant and Catholic clubs for many years, the lines between each club's ideologies have become blurred in recent years, leaving a fixture that has once again become all about football, nothing more and nothing less.

Whilst the two clubs might be referred to as the best of enemies today, it wasn't always the case. Indeed, relations between the two clubs were for many years extremely cordial, with Rangers providing the opposition in what was Celtic's very first match, in May 1888. Unsure of the quality of the opposition that would face them, Rangers selected eleven players that were a mixture of established first teamers, a handful of reserves and one or two guests. Despite this combination Celtic proved too strong on the day,

winning 5-2. The first goal in the match was scored by Neilly McCallum of Celtic, who a few months earlier had turned out for Rangers in a friendly fixture against Aston Villa and thus became the first player to have turned out for both sides of the Glasgow divide. After the match the two sides, together with club officials, sat down together for a supper and concert at St Mary's Hall, an inauspicious start to the biggest derby in the world.

ABOVE A police officer checks the time at the start of the match between arch rivals Rangers and Celtic, 1949

NOTICE

Admission will be refused to any person found carrying flags, bottles or any other missiles.

Any person found inside the ground in posse____ of flags, bottles or a____ ____issiles will be re____ ____ the premises and ____ ____uted.

Instructions ____ ____ given to the pol____ ____ these measures int____

Three months later in August 1888 the two sides met again, with Rangers getting their revenge with a 9-1 victory, although this was still a match that fell into the category of Rangers providing the opposition for their much younger rivals from across the city. The first Scottish Cup meeting between the two sides came in the first round in September 1890, with Celtic winning 1-0. In October 1888, the two clubs met in the quarter-final of the Glasgow Cup, with Celtic coming to Ibrox and recording a 6-1 victory, still their biggest ever win at Ibrox. Celtic could also claim to have got the better of their rivals in the first League meetings between the two sides, played the same season, with a 2-2 draw at Parkhead being followed by a 2-1 win for Celtic at Ibrox. Rangers, however, had the last laugh, finishing joint top of the table with Dumbarton and being declared joint champions after the two sides had drawn a deciding match.

The two sides had to wait until February 1894 before they met in the Scottish Cup Final for the first time, with Rangers registering a 3-1 win to lift the trophy for the very first time, making the victory over Celtic especially sweet.

It was not until 1898 that the relationship between Rangers and Celtic began to become strained. A crowd of 50,000 was packed into Parkhead for the New Year's Day meeting between the top two sides in the League, with the 40 or so policemen on duty unable to prevent frequent invasions by the crowd. The match itself was finally balanced at 1-1 when another invasion after seventy minutes proved impossible to clear, with the game subsequently being abandoned. Although Celtic came in for considerable criticism over their inability to control their fans, Rangers were more aggrieved over Celtic's refusal to share the gate money 50/50, as had supposedly been agreed, and received only 20%, their allotted share under the regulations of the time.

Following the Ibrox disaster of 1902, Rangers organised a four team competition involving them, Celtic, Sunderland and Everton in what became billed as the British League Cup. The trophy for the competition was the Exhibition Cup, a trophy that had been won by Rangers in 1901 after an eight team competition, beating Celtic in the final. The two Glasgow rivals met in the final of the British League Cup, with Celtic winning 3-2 after extra time, but what caused the controversy between the two sides was Celtic's refusal to put the trophy, which Rangers believed was rightfully theirs, up for annual competition. The trophy, the cause of much aggravation in 1902, remains at Parkhead to this day.

Whilst the two sides learned to tolerate each other in the years that followed, at least as far as the respective officials were concerned, the same could not be said for followers of either side. The League meeting in 1898, which as noted earlier was subsequently abandoned, was just the first in a number of matches that were disrupted, either during or after by invasions and serious and violent clashes. The most recent came after the 1980 Scottish Cup Final, which Celtic won 1-0 after extra time at Hampden Park. When the Celtic players went over to the end where their fans were congregated to celebrate, hoards of Rangers fans invaded the pitch and engaged in bitter battle on the pitch against their foes. Although both clubs were subsequently fined (a paltry £20,000 each), legislation was introduced in the shape of the Criminal Justice (Scotland) Act 1980 that went

LEFT A policemen gives advice to a fan at the local derby between Rangers and Celtic, 1949

some considerable way to removing the stain of crowd violence from the Scottish game. Future battles on the field of play have thus been confined to eleven players wearing Rangers kit and eleven Celtic counterparts.

Whilst there were several examples of players appearing for Rangers and then Celtic, with Alfie Conn during the 1970s being one of the most celebrated examples, instances of a player appearing for

BELOW A flag is raised on the pitch to welcome the teams before the infamous 'Old Firm Game'

Celtic and then Rangers are much rarer. Much of the reason for this was the religious background of the players – Celtic would sign a player irrespective of his religion, whilst for many years Rangers would only sign Protestant players. All this changed with the controversial (at least as far as Rangers fans were concerned) signing of Maurice 'Mo' Johnston, and whilst no player has played on both sides of the divide since, the two clubs are often competing to sign the same players from around the world, Catholic and Protestant alike.

If the religious overtones to the fixture have been removed, the intensity of the rivalry has not diminished. If anything it has increased; the pressure to finish the season ahead of their greatest rivals is still one that drives both Rangers and Celtic on to bigger and better things. Rangers, both inside and outside the club, still dream of emulating their rivals and getting to lift the European Champions Cup, the holy grail of club football.

Player of the year

THE SCOTTISH FOOTBALL WRITERS Association introduced their Player of the Year award in 1965, with Celtic's Billy McNeill the very first winner. The following Rangers players have won the award.

1966 – John Greig
1972 – Dave Smith
1975 – Sandy Jardine
1976 – John Greig
1978 – Derek Johnstone
1989 – Richard Gough
1992 – Ally McCoist
1993 – Andy Goram
1994 – Mark Hateley
1995 – Brian Laudrup
1996 – Paul Gascoigne
2000 – Barry Ferguson
2003 – Barry Ferguson

The players' union, the PFA, instigated its own award in 1978, voted for by all professional players. The following Rangers players have won the award.

1978 – Derek Johnstone
1992 – Ally McCoist
1993 – Andy Goram
1994 – Mark Hately
1995 – Brian Laudrup
1996 – Paul Gascoigne
2002 – Lorenzo Amoruso
2005 – Fernando Ricksen (jointly
         with John Hartson of Celtic)

BELOW Brian Laudrup winner of the Player of the Year, 1995

Provan

BORN IN FALKIRK ON 11 March 1941, Davie Provan seemed set for a lengthy and successful career at Rangers until a horrific broken leg brought his Ibrox career to an end, even if it wasn't the end of his playing career.

Davie had had to wait five years before he made his Rangers debut and it was the unfortunate broken leg sustained by Eric Caldow whilst on national duty that gave Davie his opening, appearing in the 3-1 win over Hibernian in April 1963. Davie made steady progress thereafter, winning five caps for Scotland and collecting one League title, three Scottish Cups and two League Cup winners' medals, including the treble in 1964 and also appearing in the unsuccessful European Cup Winners' Cup final of 1967.

That September, in the first Old Firm clash of the season, he suffered a broken leg in a challenge from Bertie Auld and was out of the side until December 1968. Although he returned to make eight appearances for the club, taking his tally up to 262, he was not the player he had been prior to his injury and was allowed to

ABOVE Davie Provan, back row 2nd from left

leave Ibrox, heading for England and Crystal Palace. Davie made only one appearance for the Eagles before moving on to Plymouth Argyle in March 1971 and made 129 appearances for the West Country side. He then returned to Scotland to finish his career with St Mirren.

Whilst it may have been a clash with Bertie Auld that effectively ended Davie's Ibrox career, Davie himself never bore any malice, with the pair subsequently becoming good pals and regular partners on the golf course.

Prso

MILADIN PRSO, KNOWN AS DADO, was born in Zadar in Croatia on 5 November 1974. He began his career with NK Zadar in 1991 and spent spells with Hajduk Split and NK Pazinka and was regarded as a competent if not spectacular striker.

All that was to change with his arrival in France in 1993, joining FC Rouen and two years later moving on to San Raphael. It was AS Monaco manager Jean Tigana who spotted talents in Dado that other managers had missed, signing him in 1996 and sending him out on loan to AC Ajaccio in order to get him fitter for the role he had in mind. Dado returned to Monaco in 1999 and proved a revelation, helping the club win the French title, but it was his exploits in the UEFA Champions League, particularly during the 2003-04 season, that grabbed the headlines. He was marked down as one of the most lethal strikers following a four goal blast against Deportivo de La Coruña, which Monaco won 8-3, on their way to the final that year. Unfortunately Dado was unable to find the net in the final itself and Monaco went down to a

3-0 defeat at the hands of Porto.

That summer Dado was the spearhead of the Croatian attack in the European Championships, appearing in three matches and scoring a delightful goal against France along the way. When the competition came to an end Dado was on the move again, joining Rangers on a free transfer. If he had cost a fee he would have been worth every penny, for he linked especially well with Nacho Novo and hit 18 goals (Novo got 19) as the League title

was won in spectacular fashion on the last day of the season. Earlier he had been a member of the side that won the League Cup, scoring two goals on the way to victory over Motherwell in the final.

His worth to the side is such that Alex McLeish called him his best ever signing, but success has been achieved at some considerable cost to Dado himself; at the end of every match his knees swell up and it takes a couple of days before he can train or play fully again.

Quotes

RIGHT Trevor Steven

"TO BE A RANGER IS TO SENSE THE sacred trust of upholding all that such a name means in this shrine of football. They must be true in their conception of what the Ibrox tradition seeks from them. No true Ranger has ever failed in the tradition set him." *Bill Struth*

"Our very success, gained you will agree by skill, will draw more people than ever to see it. And that will benefit many more clubs than Rangers. Let the others come after us. We welcome the chase. It is healthy for us. We will never hide from it. Never fear, inevitably we shall have our years of failure, and when they arrive, we must reveal tolerance and sanity. No matter the days of anxiety that come our way, we shall emerge stronger because of the trials to be overcome. That has been the philosophy of the Rangers since the days of the gallant pioneers." *Bill Struth*

"I was presented with the trophy in an ante-room in the bowels of the Nou Camp. You could say it was an anti-climax." *John Greig G on the 1972 European Cup Winners' Cup final.*

"The Spanish police did what was natural to them. The Rangers fans did what came naturally to them and charged." *Jock Wallace on the 1972 European Cup Winners' Cup final.*

"Sorry Mr Chairman, but this is the earliest I have been late for some time." *Ally McCoist turns up late for the chairman.*

"Ally was good enough to phone my wife and tell her that I wasn't too badly injured. I asked him what she said and his reply was 'Trevor, she can't believe I'm not playing.'" *Trevor Steven after he had been stretchered off during a game. Ally McCoist informs his wife.*

"Gazza said he was taking his wallet out on the pitch with him. I didn't understand what he was talking about until he told me that he'd read something in a paper that my mother said I would either be a footballer or a thief." *Marcos Negri*

"I have been lucky, lucky in those who were around me from the boardroom to the dressing-room. In time of stress, their unstinted support, unbroken devotion to our club and calmness in adversity eased the task of making Rangers FC the premier club in this country." *Bill Struth*

"I am of Rangers and I'll stay of Rangers until I die." *Bill Struth, manager for 34 years and director for a further two years until his death.*

Records

ABOVE Tore Andre Flo shows his worth by knocking the ball off Tommy Boyd of Celtic

Record victory
14-2 v Blairgowrie, Scottish Cup 1st round, 20/1/1934

Record defeat
0-6 v Dumbarton, Scottish League, 4/5/1892

Most League points
98 in Scottish Premier League in 2003-04 (under three points for a win), 76 in Scottish League in 1920-21 (under two points for a win)

Most League goals
118 in Scottish League in 1931-32 and 1933-34

Highest League scorer in a season –
Sam English, 44 goals in Scottish League 1931-32

Most League goals in total aggregate
Ally McCoist, 251 goals, 1983-1998

Most League appearances
Sandy Archibald, 513, 1917-34

Most capped player
Ally McCoist, 60 appearances for Scotland

Record transfer fee received
£8.5 million from Arsenal for Giovanni Van Bronckhorst, 2001

Record transfer fee paid
£12.5 million to Chelsea for Tore Andre Flo, 2000

Robertson

BORN IN DUMBARTON ON 25 February 1877, wing-half Jacky Robertson began his playing career with Morton before being spotted by Everton and signed with the Goodison Park club in 1897. He made 26 appearances in the First Division, scoring one goal but found the pace a little above him and so switched to Southampton of the Southern League the following year.

He returned to Scotland in 1899, signing with champions Rangers and made his debut against Clyde in August 1899, helping the club retain the title at the end of the season. Jacky would go on to make 120 first-team appearances for the club, winning League title medals in 1900 and 1901 and the Scottish Cup in 1903 as well as runners-up medals in 1904 and 1905.

First capped by Scotland whilst on the books of Everton, he went on to make 16 appearances for his country,

ABOVE Jacky Robertson (back row second from right)

14 of which were whilst with Rangers. He was captain of the side in their 4-1 defeat of England in 1900, a match in which Scotland wore the primrose and pink racing colours of racehorse owner Archibald Philip Primrose, Lord Rosebery. After the match Lord Rosebery was heard to remark to Jacky 'I have never seen my colours so well

sported since Ladas won the Derby.'

In 1905 Jacky accepted an invitation to become player-manager of the new Chelsea Football Club as they kicked off their campaign in the Second Division.

Jacky made 36 appearances over the next two years before switching to Glossop in a similar capacity. Jacky then went to Europe to coach MTK Budapest and Rapid Vienna. He died in 1935.

BELOW Study Support Centre, Rangers

Shaw

JOCK SHAW, APTLY known as 'Tiger', had a biting tackle and an uncompromising style that made him a feared opponent, with his fitness and speed off the mark making up for any shortcomings in his height (he stood just 5' 7") and weight (11 stone). He was already considered the finished article at fullback when Bill Struth swooped on Airdrie to pay £2,000 to bring Jock to Ibrox in July 1938, appearing in all but two of Rangers' League matches during the 1938-39 season as the League title was won.

The outbreak of the Second World War caused the abandonment of the Scottish League the following campaign but Jock helped Rangers win the hastily arranged Scottish Regional League Western Division and Emergency War

ABOVE Jock Shaw

Cup that term. Jock would go on to help Rangers win all seven wartime Leagues and a total of five cup competitions and was still the club's first choice left-back when normal League football resumed in 1946, with Rangers winning the League and also the newly introduced League Cup, the latter with a 4-0 victory over Aberdeen in April 1947. That same month Jock won the first of his four caps for Scotland, captaining the side in the 1-1 draw with England at Wembley (he was captain for all four of his appearances).

Jock would go on to win a total of four Scottish League titles, three Scottish Cups and two League Cups, figures that included the first domestic treble, achieved in 1949, and a double the following year, with only defeat in the final of the League Cup robbing Rangers of back to back trebles. Jock was already 38 years of age when the double was won and continued playing until he was 42 before switching to coaching and heading up Rangers' third team. Over the years Jock was responsible for grooming future Rangers stars such as John Greig, Sandy Jardine and Willie Henderson. He later became groundsman for the club.

Smith, Nicol

BORN ON 25 DECEMBER 1873, Nicol Smith was spotted by Rangers whilst on international duty for the junior side against Ireland in 1893 and signed up almost immediately. He was given a first team debut by Rangers soon after, selected to play at full-back in place of the injured Donald Gow and did so well Gow was unable to get his place back in the side, prompting his departure for pastures new.

Nicol meanwhile formed an uncanny understanding with fellow full-back Jock Drummond, the pair proving to be one of the best full-back partnerships the club has ever had, helping Rangers win four League titles, three Scottish Cups (including Rangers' first in the competition) and winners' medals from the Glasgow Cup, Charity Cup, Glasgow League and Exhibition Cup, these competitions being significantly more important then than they might appear now. Nicol and Drummond transferred their understanding from club level to international level, winning 25 caps for Scotland between them.

In November 1904 Nicol made his last appearance for the club before being struck down with enteric fever. His wife contracted the disease whilst nursing him and was to die just before Christmas, with Nicol suffering a relapse from the disease on 4th January and dying two days later, leaving five children orphans. The club organised a benefit match for the children, which raised nearly £400, but really the match was a chance for Rangers to say farewell to the 'Darvel Marvel'.

Smith, Walter

WALTER SMITH WAS BORN IN Carmyle on 24 February 1948 and dreamed of playing for Rangers as a youngster, although he didn't make the grade and so pursued his playing career with Dundee United whilst working part-time as an electrician. After nine years at United he moved on to Dumbarton in 1975 but returned to Dundee United two years later. A pelvic injury threatened his playing career and he was encouraged by United manager Jim McLean to pursue a coaching career.

Eventually he was appointed assistant manager to Jim McLean whilst also working with the Scotland Under-18 side, guiding them to victory in the European Youth Championship in 1982. From there he became coach to the Under-21 side and served as Alex Ferguson's assistant during the 1986 World Cup in Mexico.

That April he got a call to become Graeme Souness's assistant at Ibrox, a position he readily accepted, even though he was on the board of directors at Tannadice! He was to work

with Graeme for some five years, the partnership bringing four League titles and four League Cups to Ibrox in that time. When Graeme left to join Liverpool, the Rangers board had no hesitation in offering the position of manager to Walter Smith.

Whilst assistant managers often find the step up to manager a difficult

one to make, Walter took to the job immediately. By the time he resigned in 1998, he had become one of the club's most successful managers of all time, having lifted seven League titles, including the all important one that enabled them to register 'nine in a row' and numerous victories in the Scottish Cup and League Cup. The

1992-93 season was undoubtedly the highlight, with all three domestic trophies lifted and Rangers coming to within one match of reaching the UEFA Champions League final.

After leaving Rangers Walter resurfaced as manager of Everton in the FA Premier League but continuing financial constraints at Goodison Park made it difficult to build a side to challenge for honours and he left the club in March 2002. Two years later he resumed his partnership with Alex Ferguson at Manchester United but in December 2004 accepted the position of manager of the Scottish national team. Although he failed to take them into the 2006 World Cup Finals, he did give them back some pride and hope for the future with their performances.

Souness

BORN IN EDINBURGH ON 6 MAY 1953, Graeme Souness began his playing career at Spurs but made just one substitute appearance for the club in a UEFA Cup tie. A mixture of homesickness and his own desire for first team action quicker prompted a move to Middlesbrough where he quickly established himself as one of the brightest midfield talents in the game. He moved on to Liverpool for £350,000 in January 1978 and would go on to help the club win the League five times, the League Cup four times and the European Cup three times. In 1984 he was sold to Sampdoria for £650,000 and spent two seasons in Serie A before being lined up as player-manager of Rangers, arriving at the club in April 1986.

Right from the off Graeme announced his intention of doing things his own way, going for the best players, irrespective at times of the cost and later of their religious backgrounds – if Rangers wanted to be the best, they had to attract the best players, with a number of England internationals eventually finding their way to Ibrox.

His first match in charge, away at Hibernian in the opening game of the 1986-87 season was a fiery affair, with Graeme getting sent off for a violent foul and beginning a love hate relationship with Scottish referees that was only partially brought to an end when he retired from playing during the 1989-90 season.

OPPOSITE Walter Smith in his role as Scotland manager

BELOW Souness in action as a player

After a hesitant start to the 1986-87 campaign Rangers made progress up the table, bolstered by the arrival of the likes of Chris Woods, Graham Roberts and Terry Butcher and by the end of the campaign had won the League title for the first time in nine years and added the League Cup to the trophy cabinet.

There were other trophies too, with Graeme's time at Ibrox resulting in four League titles and four League Cups, only the Scottish FA Cup proving elusive with defeat in the final of 1988-89 the closest they came during this time.

As well as Woods, Roberts and Butcher, other England international players who signed for Rangers were Trevor Francis, Trevor Steven, Gary Stevens and Ray Wilkins, alongside others who had plied their trade in the English game such as Mark Falco and Richard Gough. This reversed the trend of previous decades when the best Scottish players had headed south of the border to play.

RIGHT A Pensive Graeme Souness

BELOW Souness and Ally McCoist celebrate with a young supporter after winning the Skol Cup, 1990

It was the signing of Mo Johnston that astonished the most, with Rangers seemingly signing a Catholic player for the first time in their history, but whilst Rangers under Graeme Souness were winning honours, who was to argue.

In 1988 Graeme was instrumental in bringing David Murray into the club, pairing up with the millionaire to buy a controlling interest in Rangers. Despite his vested interest in Rangers, there were still those who believed his heart was still at Liverpool and when, in April 1991 his former club invited him to take over as manager, he jumped at the chance. Later events were to prove he may have made the wrong decision, and subsequent appointments at Southampton, Galatasaray, Torino, Benfica, Blackburn Rovers and Newcastle United have been somewhat bare as far as silverware is concerned.

Whilst he may have left Rangers too early into his managerial career, there is no doubt Graeme was almost single-handedly responsible for dragging the club back on to the top table of Scottish football. Had he remained at Ibrox for longer, he may even have converted consistent domestic success into European glory. His heart and Liverpool ensured we will never know.

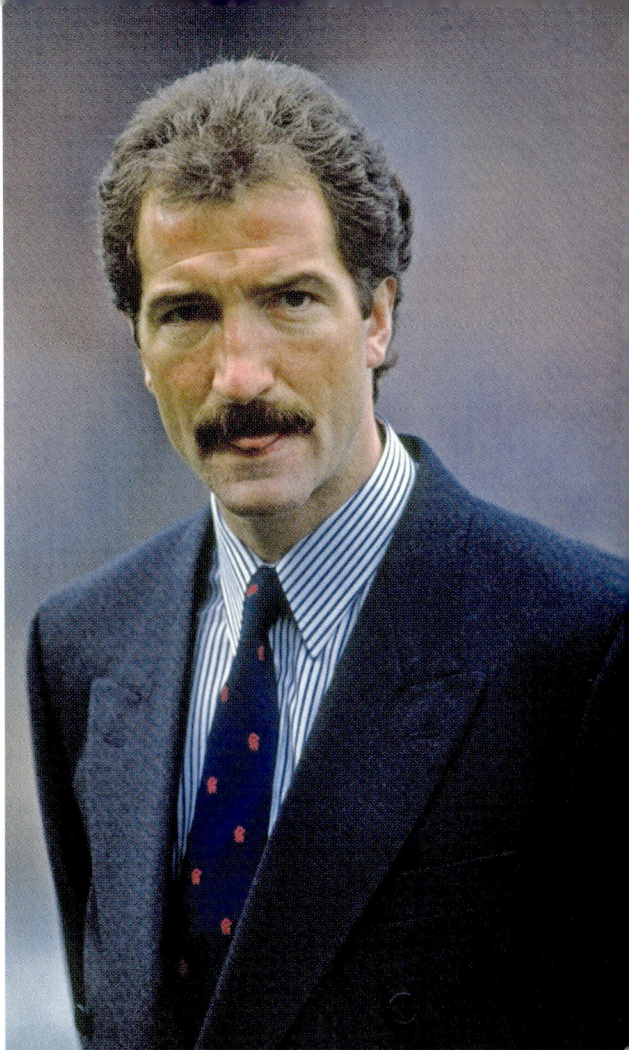

Stein

BORN IN PHILIPSTOUN IN WEST Lothian on 10 May 1947, Colin Stein began his career with Hibernian and quickly developed into one of the best centre-forwards in the Scottish game, prompting considerable attention from a number of other clubs. Everton believed they had got their man with a £90,000 offer in October 1968, but Rangers were able to hijack this deal, paying £100,000 even though a number of Hibernian directors were not prepared to sell their star player to a rival Scottish club.

Their fears were to be proved right, for a week after netting a hat-trick on his debut against Arbroath, Colin netted a second hat-trick against his old club in the 6-1 victory, the presence of Colin adding some 20,000 to the gate.

For many years it was believed that the equalising goal he scored against Celtic on New Year's Day 1971 was indirectly responsible for causing the crush that left 66 dead, the inference being that those who were trying to leave the ground heard the roar of the crowd acclaiming the goal and turned back to see the celebrations, but later evidence proved all of those who died did so some considerable time after the final whistle.

Whilst Rangers were a struggling force domestically during Colin's time with the club, he was one of the key players who brought the European Cup Winners' Cup to Ibrox in 1972, scoring one of the goals in the 3-2 win over Dinamo Moscow. That proved to be a virtual swansong for Colin, for he was sold to Coventry City for £90,000 in October 1972. He made 83 appearances for the Highfield Road club, scoring 22 goals, before returning to Ibrox for a second spell in February 1975. Whilst his initial games were not as goal laden as his first, he did score some vital strikes, including the one that clinched the title with a 1-1 draw against Hibernian. The following season, 1975-76 he collected his second League Cup winners' medal (he had been a member

of the 1970-71 side) with a 1-0 victory over Celtic, the only domestic medals he got his hands on.

Competition for places was at its keenest and he was allowed to go on loan to Kilmarnock during the 1977-78 campaign, eventually leaving Rangers at the end of the season. He won 21 caps for Scotland, all but four whilst with Rangers, and scored ten goals.

Struth

RIGHT Bill Struth, former secretary who is buried close to his beloved club at Craigton Cemetery

BILL STRUTH WAS ALREADY working at Ibrox as a trainer when the tragic death of William Wilton was announced. The club decided on as painless a transition at Ibrox as was possible and appointed Bill to the position of secretary-manager in May 1920, a position he was to hold for the next 34 years.

Born in Edinburgh in 1873, he had been a stonemason and professional athlete before pursuing an interest in sports training, joining Clyde FC as trainer in 1908 and then switching to Ibrox in a similar capacity in 1914. Neither William Wilton nor Bill Struth worried much about tactics, but whilst Wilton was the club's father figure, Bill Struth imposed the discipline.

He established a network of scouts around the country, a network whose job it was to inform him of any players the club might be interested in signing and any gossip relating to those they had already signed! And whilst William Wilton had introduced a dress code into the club, it was Bill Struth who saw to it that it was enforced.

According to legend, he would look out of the window of his flat that over-looked Copland Road observing the players arriving for training – if even one arrived with his hands in his pockets, he would be summoned to the office and told to walk the street again, this time with his hands by his side!

Whilst the discipline within the club was strict, the rewards were great. Bill Struth insisted on the best of everything for Rangers, which meant travelling first class to every fixture and the best hotels and rooms when staying overnight. He himself kept numerous suits in his office and would sometimes change them three times a day!

This attention to detail brought with it immense success – eighteen League titles, including a then unprecedented five in a row between 1927 and 1931. It was Bill Struth who delivered the club's first 'double' in 1928 and the first treble in 1949. He was appointed a director of the club in 1947, adding this role to that of secretary-manager. He maintained this role until his resignation as secretary-manager in the summer of 1954 but remained on the board until his death, aged 81, in September 1956.

Thornton

WILLIE THORNTON SPENT HIS entire career in football, turning to coaching and management after his own playing career came to an end, and both began and ended his career giving service to Rangers.

Born in Winchburg in West Lothian on 3 March 1920, he signed with Rangers as an amateur in March 1936 and was upgraded to the professional ranks the following year. By then he had already made his first team debut, appearing five times in what would ultimately become Rangers' title winning season of 1936-37.

Thereafter he became a virtual regular, making 36 appearances in the title winning season of 1938-39, the last before the outbreak of the Second World War, scoring 23 goals. Although centre-forwards were supposed to be big and mean, Willie was never even booked during his career. In all he won four League titles, three Scottish Cups and three League Cups during his time with Rangers, figures that would have been considerably higher had the war not robbed him of some seven years of foot-

ball. He did, however, win the Military Medal during the conflict for his part in actions in Sicily in 1943.

He retired from playing in 1954 having made 432 appearances for Rangers and scored 255 goals. He then took over as manager of Dundee United, a position he held for five years before replacing Davie Meiklejohn as manager of Partick Thistle. Willie spent nine years with the club before returning to Rangers to become assistant to David White and then Willie Waddell. He died after a brief illness on 26 August 1991.

Top Ten

The ten biggest fees paid out are for the following players:

£12.5 million	Tore Andre Flo (Chelsea)
£6.5 million	Michael Ball (Everton)
£5.8 million	Mikel Arteta (Barcelona)
£5.5 million	Andrei Kanchelskis (Fiorentina)
£5 million	Arthur Numan (PSV Eindhoven)
£5 million	Giovanni Van Bronckhorst (Feyenoord)
£4.5 million	Ronald De Boer (Barcelona)
£4.5 million	Barry Ferguson (Blackburn Rovers)
£4.3 million	Paul Gascoigne (Lazio)
£4.3 million	Bert Konterman (Feyenoord)

The ten biggest fees received are for the following players:

£8.5 million	Giovanni Van Bronckhorst (Arsenal)
£8 million	Jean-Alain Boumsong (Newcastle United)
£6.75 million	Tore Andre Flo (Sunderland)
£6.5 million	Barry Ferguson (Blackburn Rovers)
£5 million	Trevor Steven (Olympique Marseille)
£4.75 million	Claudio Reyna (Sunderland)
£3.75 million	Duncan Ferguson (Everton)
£3.75 million	Gabriel Amato (Cremio)
£3.5 million	Paul Gascoigne (Middlesbrough)
£3.4 million	Stephane Guivarc'h (Auxerre)

BELOW Barry Ferguson in action

Unforgettable

THERE WAS NEVER ANY doubt that Rangers would win the League title in 1898-99, recording what is still the only 100% record in a major League competition in the world and finishing ten points ahead of their nearest rivals Hearts, with 18 games played and only two points available for a win. There have been fifty other title wins, some won by a considerable margin, others on the slenderest, but none have ever quite matched the wins of 2002-03 and 2004-05 for sheer drama.

The 2002-03 season went right down to the wire, with Rangers neck and neck with reigning champions Celtic for virtually the whole of the season. Indeed,

ABOVE Passionate Rangers fans

so close was the race that after Rangers had lost 2-1 at home to Celtic with just four games to go, the destination of the title was still not guaranteed. Going into the final game of the season, the two

ABOVE The impressive gates at Ibrox

RIGHT Rangers fans during the Scottish Cup Final between Celtic and Rangers, 2002

Kilmarnock. The second half of both matches was played out with equal drama, Celtic scoring and then missing a penalty whilst Rangers were moving further ahead. A fifth Rangers goal was greeted with the news Celtic had gone 4-0 up – another Celtic goal would give them the title, but as the Rangers match entered virtually the final minute, there was still time for Rangers to get a penalty of their own, which was duly despatched by Mikel Arteta. The final whistle went at both grounds, Celtic having won 4-0 and Rangers 6-1 to clinch the title for the fiftieth time in their history by just one goal.

clubs were level on points and goal difference, with Rangers slightly ahead by virtue of having scored more goals than their rivals. This meant that Rangers, away at Dunfermline, had to equal or better whatever Celtic managed at Kilmarnock.

By half time both Glasgow rivals were ahead, Rangers 3-1 up against Dunfermline and Celtic 2-0 in front of

If that was close, then the events of 2004-05 were equally dramatic. Indeed, the events of the final day of the season have entered into folklore as 'Helicopter Sunday'. Going into the final match of the season, Celtic led the table by two points from Rangers and were due to play at Motherwell, where former

Rangers legend Terry Butcher was manager. Rangers meanwhile were the visitors to a Hibernian side that were chasing third spot in the table and with it a place in the UEFA Cup, so they had their own desire to perform well. A goal from Nacho Novo just before the hour mark proved to be the only goal at Easter Road, so thoughts immediately turned to what was happening at Motherwell. With Chris Sutton having scored for Celtic after just half an hour the omens did not look good, with a young Motherwell side battling hard but getting little or no reward for their efforts. Then, as the Motherwell and Celtic match headed towards the injury time, Scott McDonald scored with an overhead kick. News of this goal was still being cheered at Easter Road when Scott McDonald nipped in to score a second and decisive goal against Celtic with literally the last kick of the game. Having been chasing the League title all season, Rangers finally got on top in the final minute! So sure were the football authorities that Celtic would win the title, the helicopter carrying the trophy was already on its way to Motherwell for presentation to Celtic, only to have to turn around and head for Edinburgh at the last moment!

Van Bronckhorst

BORN IN ROTTERDAM ON 5 February 1975, Giovanni Van Bronckhorst is assured his place in the Rangers record books for being one of the most costly players brought in and the most expensive transfer out again, at least for the foreseeable future.

He began his career with RKC Waalwijk but made his name with Feyenoord, joining the club in 1994 and spending four years with the Rotterdam club. When Dutch manager Dick Advocaat took over at Ibrox he targeted a number of fellow Dutchmen to join him at the club, paying Feyenoord £5 million to bring Giovanni to Ibrox. He made his debut in the UEFA Cup tie against Shelbourne and played a significant part in the comeback from 3-0 down to winning 5-3, scoring one of the goals.

Used as an attack minded midfielder, Giovanni would go on to score 22 goals for the club, including 13 in the League, three in the Scottish Cup, one in the League Cup, three in the

ABOVE Giovanni Van Bronckhorst on one of his foward runs

Champions League and two in the UEFA Cup before a record-breaking £8.5 move to Arsenal in the summer of 2001. By then he had two League titles, a Scottish Cup and League Cup winners' medals to his name. He struggled to hold down a regular place at Arsenal, prompting a further move to Barcelona in 2003. He is, however, a regular within the Dutch national side, having been switched to a more defensive role, and had 56 caps to his name before the 2006 World Cup kicked off.

Venters

ALEX VENTERS JOINED RANGERS from Cowdenbeath and made his debut on 25 November 1933 in a 3-1 win over Falkirk at Ibrox. He would go on to make 15 League appearances that season, scoring five goals as the League title was retained. Despite his growing importance to the League side, he made only one appearance in the Scottish Cup, the 1st round match against Blairgowrie when he scored twice in the 14-2 win.

He made up for this disappointment the following season, helping Rangers to the double with ten goals in his 28 appearances. Although he did not score during the successful cup campaign he did appear in all seven matches, helping the club lift the trophy with victory over Hamilton Academicals in the final. Alex helped Rangers win a further two League titles and the Scottish Cup before the outbreak of the Second World War and would make a final four appearances for the League side when normal football resumed in 1946.

By the time he left the club he had scored 102 League goals and a further 53 in the various wartime Leagues, making him one of the most prolific inside-forwards the club ever had. When his playing career came to an end he went to work in the printing industry where he died at the premature age of just 45 in 1959.

RIGHT Excited fans at Ibrox

Waddell

WILLIE WADDELL'S NAME HAS become synonymous with the ambitious rebuilding of Ibrox, after the tragic events of 1971, into one of the finest stadiums in the country, but he gave the club exceptional service in a wide variety of other roles.

Born in 1921, Willie had first been associated with Rangers as a player, joining the club in May 1938 and becoming an integral part of the side in the immediate post-war period when he supplied the crosses for the likes of Willie Thornton that would eventually bring four League titles, two Scottish Cups and three League Cups, having already won a variety of wartime League and cups during the conflict. Willie also won 17 caps for Scotland before his retirement from playing in the summer of 1956, having made 517 appearances for the club.

ABOVE Willie Waddell leaps over the challenge from Partick Thistle's Bobby Gibb

After a spell in journalism, Willie returned to football as manager of Kilmarnock and set about turning the club's fortunes around. By 1960 he had

ABOVE Willie Waddell

years later he was brought back to Rangers to replace David White and the following year delivered the first trophy in six years in the shape of the League Cup. The Ibrox disaster, together with his own belief that the players would be better working more closely with a younger man on the training field saw Willie Waddell start to take a back seat role. Whilst he may not have had as much day to day contact with the players, his influence could be seen as Ibrox became transformed.

Although Willie resigned as team manager in 1972 his work was still not done, continuing to serve the club as managing director, general manager and then vice chairman before his death in 1992. Before he died, he saw Ibrox convert itself from an elliptical death trap into a thoroughly modern and impressive stadium, a lasting legacy.

lifted them into the top reaches of the League finishing runners-up behind Hearts. Kilmarnock were to finish runners-up a further three times in four years, all behind Rangers, before finally lifting the title in 1964-65. Four

Wallace

JOCK WALLACE IS THE only man to have managed Rangers twice, with both spells in charge ending somewhat unceremoniously. Born in Wallyford on 6 September 1935, Jock signed with Blackpool as an amateur but was released without ever having played for the first team. Undeterred Jock went elsewhere and played in goal for Workington Town, Airdrie and West Bromwich Albion as well as a couple of non-League clubs before being appointed player-manager of Berwick Rangers. It was Jock who did most to deny the Rangers strike force in that infamous Scottish Cup tie in 1967, but he did not see that as the pinnacle of his career, working hard to get Berwick challenging for promotion.

Eventually Jock's efforts were rewarded with a move to a bigger club, being appointed assistant manager of Hearts. There the higher profile brought him to the attention of Rangers once again, with Willie Waddell offering Jock the role of coach at Ibrox in June 1970.

ABOVE Jock Wallace, a great leader and motivator

He worked the players hard, demanding the highest possible levels of fitness and stamina for the challenges ahead and looking to close the gap between them and Celtic.

In 1972 Willie Waddell decided to move into more of an administrative role at the club (he was preoccupied with rebuilding Ibrox into one of the finest stadiums in the country) and Jock was appointed team manager, taking over a side that had just won the European Cup Winners' Cup. Jock set about making Rangers great again, winning the Scottish Cup in 1973 and the League title in 1975, Rangers' first in eleven years. The following year he won every domestic honour, the League, League Cup and Scottish Cup, a treble he was to repeat in 1978.

Despite this latter success, Jock Wallace resigned soon after, with neither club nor manager revealing the full reasons as to why he had left the club, although it was later claimed that he and Willie Waddell had clashed over player trans-fers Jock had identified as necessary to the club but which Waddell wouldn't sanction because it would have diverted funds away from the rebuilding of the stadium.

Jock Wallace went south of the border and took over at Leicester City, taking them into the top flight and the semi-finals of the FA Cup before returning to Scotland to take over at Motherwell in 1982. The following October, following the departure of John Greig (who had replaced Jock Wallace in 1978), Rangers once again turned to Jock Wallace. His second spell in charge brought further success in the shape of consecutive League Cup victories, but it was Rangers' inability to mount a serious title challenge that brought increasing pressure. The arrival of a new chief executive in the shape of David Holmes, who may already have had Graeme Souness lined up as player-manager, meant Jock's days in charge were numbered and he was sacked in April 1986. He later went to Spain to manage Seville and was a manager and then director of Colchester United before his death on 24 July 1996 from motor neurone disease.

LEFT Jock Wallace walks out of the Ibrox tunnel

Wilkins

WHEN GRAEME SOUNESS PAID Paris St Germain £250,000 for Ray Wilkins in November 1987, there were many who questioned the move for a player already the wrong side of 30 and known for being, at times, an unadven-turous player, opting for the safe sideways ball rather than look for a more telling through ball. Graeme Souness knew what he was buying and in the space of two years Rangers fans came to appreciate what it was Ray brought to the team.

Born in Hillingdon on 14 September 1956, Ray had begun his

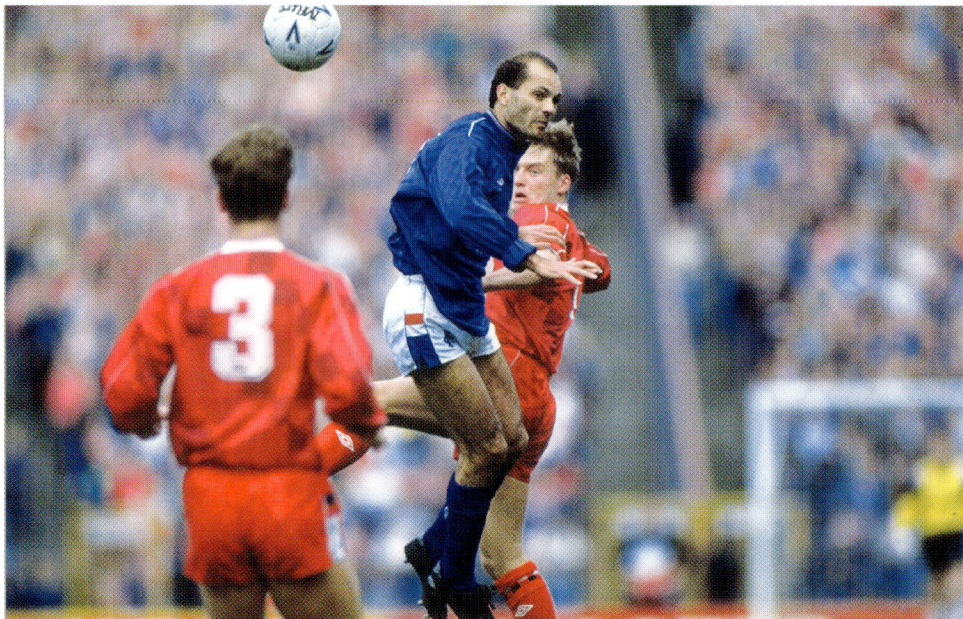

career with Chelsea, being made captain at the age of 18. Later moves to Manchester United and AC Milan brought him numerous honours and awards, including 84 caps for England, and it was this experience that prompted Graeme Souness to sign him in 1987. Ray's Ibrox career was to last two years, bringing with it the League title in 1989 and 1990 and the League Cup in 1989 before he moved to London to join QPR. As well as the medals, however, came a reputation that was enhanced during his time at the club; many Rangers fans hold him to be one of the most skilful midfield players they have had the honour of watching.

BELOW Ray Wilkins playing for England against Scotland, 1985

Xmas day

RIGHT A Snowman wearing the Rangers strip

WHILST FOOTBALL MATCHES played on Christmas Day were taken as part and parcel of the festivities in England for many a year, with the last of these being played in 1958, in Scotland these were only played if Christmas Day fell on a Saturday, and then only as part of the normal fixture list. Thus Christmas Day matches continued in Scotland for some 13 years after they had been halted in England. Here therefore is a list of matches played by Rangers on Christmas Day. With the exception of the 1880 fixture, all of these were League matches, with the fixtures in 1943 and 1945 being wartime League fixtures. The Dumbarton fixture of 1880 was a Scottish Cup quarter-final.

Year	Opponents	Venue	Score	Year	Opponents	Venue	Score
1880	Dumbarton	Home	1-3	1943	Third Lanark	Home	3-1
1897	Dundee	Home	5-0	1945	Clyde	Home	3-1
1909	Falkirk	Away	1-3	1947	Dundee	Away	3-1
1915	Falkirk	Home	1-0	1948	Falkirk	Away	2-2
1920	Clyde	Away	3-1	1954	Hibernian	Away	1-2
1926	Dundee United	Away	0-2	1965	Dunfermline Athletic	Home	2-3
1934	Falkirk	Home	1-0				
1937	St Johnstone	Away	5-1	1971	Hibernian	Away	1-0

Young

A BIG DEFENDER, STANDING SOME 6' 2" tall and weighing in at 15 stone at his prime, George Young was a colossus for Rangers both on and off the field and an uncompromising and inspirational leader. Born in Grangemouth in 1922, George signed with Rangers as an amateur in 1937 and was upgraded to the professional ranks in 1941.

Whilst centre-half would appear to have been his natural position, the presence of Willie Woodburn in that position meant George was switched to right-back but together the pair formed part of one of the most successful defences in the domestic game. Not for nothing was it known as the 'Iron Curtain' defence, the foundation upon which Rangers were to win six League titles whilst George was in the side. There was also four Scottish Cup and two League Cup victories to savour,

ABOVE A policeman helping George Young from the pitch after Scotland beat England 3-1 at Wembley

with George scoring twice from the penalty spot in the 1949 Scottish Cup Final against Clyde.

Known as 'Corky' throughout his career on account of the lucky champagne cork he carried around with him, George also won 53 caps for Scotland, captaining the side on 48 occasions, indicative of how highly he was regarded at both club and international level. His playing career came to an end in the summer of 1957 and he went on to manage Third Lanark for three years.

ZZZ Moments to forget

WHILST RANGERS' HISTORY HAS, for the most part, been laden with success there have still been moments that would be better forgotten. Some of these have come in the full gaze of the watching football world, such as the 7-1 defeat inflicted by Celtic in the League Cup Final in 1957, the very first time the two sides had contested the final. Whilst Rangers have beaten and lost to Celtic in many cup finals since, neither side has managed to register a victory quite as emphatic as that 7-1 scoreline, something Rangers would love to repay with interest.

As humiliating as that defeat was, it still does not compare with the events a little under ten years later. By the time January 1967 came around, Rangers were still playing catch up with reigning champions Celtic, having already lost to them in the League Cup Final 1-0 the previous October. On 28 January thoughts turned to the Scottish FA Cup, with Rangers drawn away to that other Rangers, Berwick. A record attendance of 13,365 was packed into Shielfield Park, fully expecting Rangers (the Glasgow variety) to rack up a handsome goal tally and progress into the second round.

Things did not go their way, however, for the Berwick goalkeeper performed heroics to keep out everything Rangers

threw at him and Sammy Reid popped up at the other end to score the only goal of the game. It was the first time in 30 years Rangers had gone out of the competition at the first round stage and the first time in the twentieth century they had lost to a team from outside the Scottish top flight. Rangers chairman John Lawrence was so disgusted with the performance he promised that some of the players would never play for the club again, which turned out to be true for two of them. Meanwhile, national attention was focused on the previously unknown Berwick Rangers players. Whilst Reid may have scored the only goal, the undoubted star performer for Berwick Rangers was goalkeeper Jock Wallace, later to become Rangers manager on two occasions!

Exactly eleven years after the defeat, Rangers were again drawn away to Berwick Rangers in the corresponding round (following re-organisation of the cup for the 1971-72 season, Rangers now entered at the third round); this time Rangers made sure the result went by the form book, winning 4-2.

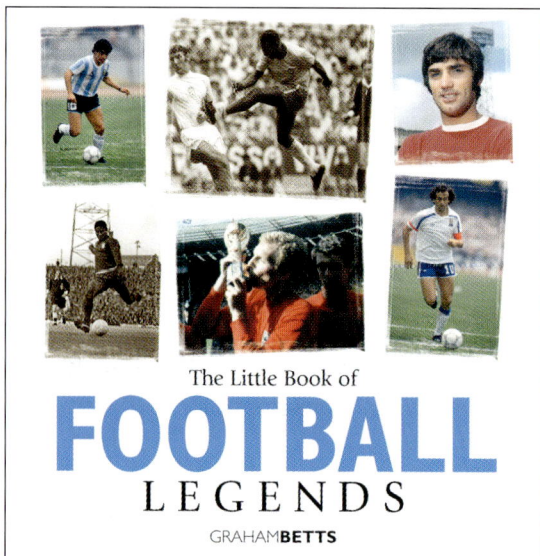

The pictures in this book were provided courtesy of the following:

GETTY IMAGES
101 Bayham Street, London NW1 0AG

EMPICS
www.empics.com

Book design and artwork by Newleaf Design

Published by Green Umbrella

Publishers Jules Gammond & Vanessa Gardner

Picture Research by Ellie Charleston

Written by Graham Betts